ANN-MARIE POWELL'S

PLANS FOR **SMALL** GARDENS

DESIGN • BUILD • MAINTAIN • ENJOY

PAVILION

First published in Great Britain in
2012 by
PAVILION BOOKS
10 Southcombe Street
London, W14 0RA

An imprint of the Anova Books
Company Ltd

Design and layout © Pavilion, 2011
Text © Ann-Marie Powell, 2011
Illustrations © Ann-Marie Powell, 2011
Photography © Rachel Warne, 2011

Commissioning editor:
Emily Preece-Morrison
Designer: Paul Tilby
Editor: Nina Sharman
Indexer: Sandra Shotter
Jacket designed by Georgina Hewitt

All photographs by Rachel Warne,
except page 174, which is by
Katie Inglis.

ISBN 978-1-86205-876-7

A CIP catalogue record for this
book is available from the
British Library.

10 9 8 7 6 5 4 3 2 1

Reproduction by Rival Colour, UK
Printed and bound by
Craft Print Ltd, Singapore

www.anovabooks.com

CONTENTS

Introduction 4

Urban Garden 8

Edible Garden 24

Romantic Front Garden 40

English Country Garden 50

Suntrap Garden 66

Low-maintenance Garden . . .82

Rustic Family Garden 96

Night Garden 116

Terraced Garden 132

Minimalist Garden 148

Techniques 161

Index 183

List of Suppliers 188

Glossary 190

Further Reading 191

Acknowledgements 192

INTRODUCTION

Whether in town or in the middle of the country, looking out on to your garden can be an overwhelming experience, stirring up a wealth of emotions. It may be that looking out at your garden leaves you excited, depressed or simply confused, but there's no denying that any outdoor space is precious, no matter what size it is. Once built, even the smallest garden plays an important part in extending the useable space of your property, becoming an outdoor room to enhance you and your family's quality of life.

Often, as you stare out from your window to consider the outdoor space beyond, a bout of head-scratching will ensue, culminating in a list of befuddling questions: what to do with the space, what to include, where to begin, what and how to build features, and what to plant?

It is important not to feel overwhelmed or disheartened by all of these considerations; the plot of land outside of your house is essentially a combination of elements, which, when combined together, can create the perfect garden to suit your needs. The secret to creating a successful garden, particularly when space is at a premium, is to consider those things that are most important to you, such as the individual characteristics of soil type, or how the surrounding environment might affect your garden. Don't be tempted to include the wide lawn, tall trees and deep planting borders associated with larger gardens; attempting to reduce all of these elements to fit in to a small space will result in an uncohesive muddle where nothing seems quite large enough and your garden begins to feel crowded. Concentrate on those elements that suit your personal style, and that lend themselves to your lifestyle, with its possible time constraints, the style of your house and the surroundings that your garden lies within. Once you've considered these factors you can develop the essential elements of your garden to create maximum impact.

LEFT *Statement plants work well in small gardens. Choose architectural foliage, long-flowering blooms or bold flowers. Border gaps are a great way of growing vegetables in the tiniest of plots.*

RIGHT *With careful design, even the most awkward of urban spaces can become a garden, offering a tranquil oasis in which to rest the eye and recharge the soul.*

Remember that less is sometimes more. Your garden can be limited to only a few elements but still be strikingly effective; a low-maintenance, minimalist terrace surrounded by a few carefully selected structural plants and sculptural elements – which change through seasons, weather and light – can be a wonderful place to relax in or contemplate from indoors. Whilst vegetables can be mixed through wider plantings, your small space garden can become an urban potager, or a family friendly garden built to attract wildlife. The choice is ultimately yours.

ABOVE *Linking hard landscaping colours to your plant palette is a wonderful way to create a cohesive whole.*

ABOVE *This city garden echoes the bold lines and architectural shapes of its urban surroundings.*

Successful gardens rarely happen on their own, they are usually carefully planned and designed in order to maximize their potential. This is extremely important in the small garden, which is open to intense scrutiny; in a small space, the whole garden can be viewed and assessed in one glance. As a rule of thumb, the smaller the garden, the more important good design becomes. Keep things simple, stick to one overall style, choose complementary materials and plants, and never be tempted to cram in more features than your space will allow. Planning the whole garden in advance is crucial to its success.

An important exercise is to create a wish list of what you'd ideally like your garden to include. Next,

realistically consider how many features your garden will have room for, what time you will need to look after your garden and, equally important, what budget you have to construct your garden. Drawing up a scale plan of your ultimate garden is not only a good way of working through your planned inclusions, it will also help you to identify the features that are essential as well as those that you can live without. A plan will also allow you to work out practical sizes for seating areas, border size and storage options too. Finally, a scale presentation plan illustrating the end result of your space will allow you to realistically consider the space you have to work with and what quantities of materials you will need – always remember that plans indicate space, and material

ABOVE *Exterior lighting transforms your garden after dark, and it also extends the hours you can spend enjoying it.*

ABOVE *Even a tiny seating area will allow you to relax and enjoy the sights, sounds and scents of your garden.*

selections and initial plant purchase size can be up or downgraded depending on how much you have to spend.

Most often, particularly if this small outdoor space is your first, deciding upon what you actually like can be the biggest hurdle to overcome. And this is where I hope this book will help. Hopefully, within one of the ten variously styled gardens included, you'll find a style that suits you, elements from different gardens that you might like to combine, or a starting point from which to interpret and develop a garden that is personal to you.

Once you've decided upon the style you'd like to take, the garden will begin to unfold. In these pages you'll find helpful advice on choosing materials and plants, building the garden yourself, or employing professionals to carry

out the work for you. There are also comprehensive material and plant lists for each project, which will take the mystery out of the sometimes daunting prospect of building your own garden and tackling various horticultural techniques. However you choose to interpret these various tried and tested garden projects, and whatever style you choose, be confident enough to go with your instincts and enjoy the journey. After all, gardens are for people, not just for plants, and though the gardens within these pages were designed and constructed for others, they will hopefully offer you the inspiration and help to develop a garden that is distinctly yours.

Ann-Marie Powell

URBAN GARDEN

PLANNING THE GARDEN

Small, overlooked, lacking in privacy; often noisy, with awkward shapes and difficult nooks and crannies – urban gardens are, generally, frustrating! Throw into the mix a young family with three small children – who want space to play in, ride bicycles and grow their own plants – and the demands upon this urban plot become extremely high.

Whether a roof garden, a balcony, an awkward space between house and street or a communal space, an urban outdoor area or patch of ground is, in many ways, infinitely more precious than a small space in a rural environment, which is often surrounded by the luxury of trees, fields and flowers. As well as the owners themselves, passers by, neighbours and wildlife can all benefit from an urban garden, whatever its size. Even the most challenging of spaces can be transformed into an interesting, cultivated oasis, amidst the concrete grey buildings and high-octane atmosphere of the city. Have a go.

DESIGN ELEMENTS

On this project, a long, dark, narrow corridor at the side of the house (the site of the front door) separated this garden into two distinct spaces; one at the front of the property, intended for adult socializing, and a family space at the rear. The key to unlocking the space and making the garden appear larger was to transform the dull corridor into an inviting green pathway. Once greenery was added, it became a plant-lined walkway, an area where the children could run up and down. Viewed from inside, window boxes, crammed with foliage and flowers, add further interest. What was once a functional access route soon became an integral part of the outdoor space, encasing the house in colourful foliage, and linking the front and rear gardens together.

RIGHT *Laying decks at the same level as interior flooring makes a wonderfully smooth transition from inside to out.*

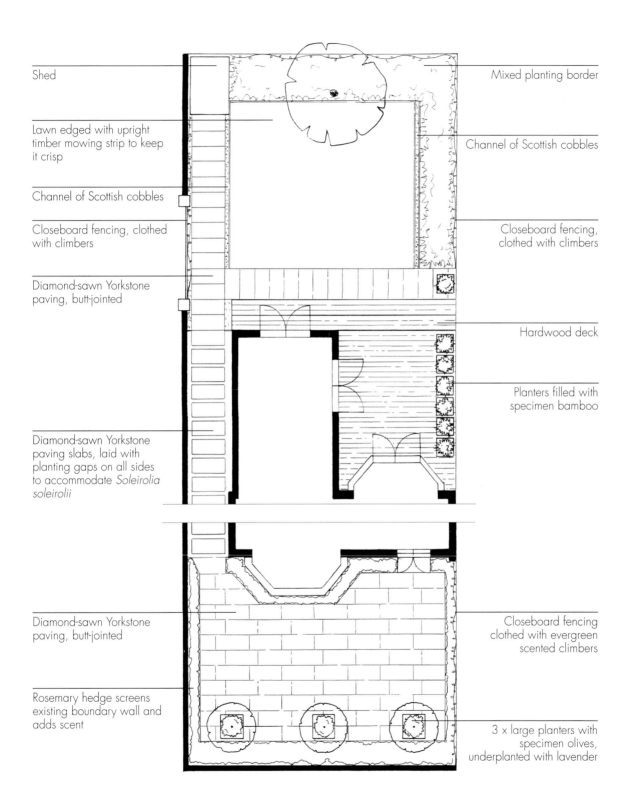

Shed

Lawn edged with upright timber mowing strip to keep it crisp

Channel of Scottish cobbles

Closeboard fencing, clothed with climbers

Diamond-sawn Yorkstone paving, butt-jointed

Diamond-sawn Yorkstone paving slabs, laid with planting gaps on all sides to accommodate *Soleirolia soleirolii*

Diamond-sawn Yorkstone paving, butt-jointed

Rosemary hedge screens existing boundary wall and adds scent

Mixed planting border

Channel of Scottish cobbles

Closeboard fencing, clothed with climbers

Hardwood deck

Planters filled with specimen bamboo

Closeboard fencing clothed with evergreen scented climbers

3 x large planters with specimen olives, underplanted with lavender

WHAT YOU WILL NEED

HARD LANDSCAPING

Skip

Concrete (ballast, ordinary Portland cement, water)

DECKING

100 x 100mm (4 x 4in) pressure-treated timber posts for decking frame

100 x 50mm (4 x 2in) pressure-treated timber joists

90mm (3½in) decking frame screws

145 x 20mm (5¾ x ¾in) smooth Balau hardwood decking boards

60mm (2⅓in) decking screws – 28 screws per square metre

Concrete to support frame posts: ballast and ordinary Portland cement (5:1 ratio) plus water

PAVING

MOT type 1 scalpings

Diamond-sawn Yorkstone in bespoke sizes

Bull-nosed pieces of diamond-sawn Yorkstone for steps

Lithofin Stain Stop

Sharp sand and cement laying mix for paving

Soft sand and cement mix (4:1 ratio) for pointing

LAWN

Scottish cobbles as lawn edging behind timber edge strip

Balau timber edging

Treated pointed pegs to support timber edging

Topsoil

Rolawn Medallion turf

HORIZONTAL TRELLIS

40 x 10mm (1½ x ⅜in) cedar timber

75 x 75mm (3 x 3in) pressure-treated timber posts

50mm (2in) external grade screws

Fence posts (studded and resin-fixed to the top of existing wall)

All trellis to be capped with 70 x 45mm (2¾ x 1¾in) top rail

WALLS

Paint

LIGHTING

Hunza adjustable spotlights in powder-coated finish

Hunza wall downlights in powder-coated finish

IRRIGATION

Micro irrigation with computerized timber (available in kit form from garden centres and Internet suppliers)

NB Measure your garden carefully in order to establish the quantities required to suit your particular outdoor space. All lighting to be installed by a qualified electrician.

PLANTING

Vine eyes; planters; window boxes

Compost; well-rotted horse manure; Fish, blood and bone fertilizer

Polystyrene chippings for drainage; gravel for mulch

FRONT GARDEN

Olea europaea specimens

Phyllostachys aurea

Rosmarinus officinalis 'Miss Jessop's Upright'

SIDE RETURN PASSAGEWAY

Soleirolia soleirolii

Trailing *Hedera helix*

REAR GARDEN

Alchemilla mollis

Anemanthele lessoniana

Aquilegia 'Ruby Port'

Deschampsia cespitosa 'Golden Dew'

Digitalis ferruginea

Gaura lindheimeri

Helleborus orientalis hybrids

Hemerocallis 'Ice Carnival'

Isotoma 'Dark Blue'

Nemesia 'Confetti'

Phyllostachys nigra

Platycodon grandiflorus

Sorbus aria

Trachelospermum jasminoides

NB Plants are usually grouped in numbers of 3, 5 and 7, but the numbers you choose should be determined by the size of your garden.

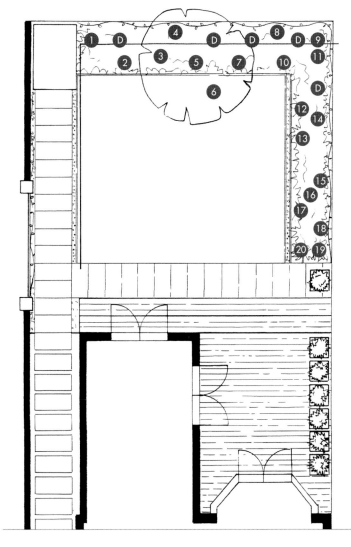

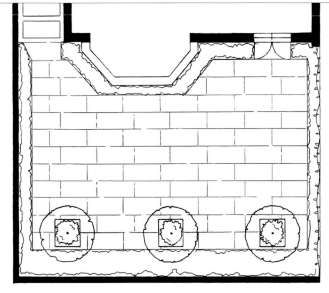

PLANTING PLAN

① *Deschampsia cespitosa* 'Golden Dew'

② *Helleborus orientalis* hybrids

③ *Isotoma* 'Dark Blue'

④ *Anemanthele lessoniana*

⑤ *Alchemilla mollis*

⑥ *Sorbus aria*

⑦ *Gaura lindheimeri*

⑧ *Aquilegia* 'Ruby Port'

⑨ *Aquilegia* 'Ruby Port'

⑩ *Helleborus orientalis* hybrids

⑪ *Anemanthele lessoniana*

⑫ *Alchemilla mollis*

⑬ *Hemerocallis* 'Ice Carnival'

⑭ *Aquilegia* 'Ruby Port'

⑮ *Deschampsia cespitosa* 'Golden Dew'

⑯ *Nemesia* 'Confetti'

⑰ *Alchemilla mollis*

⑱ *Hemerocallis* 'Ice Carnival'

⑲ *Helleborus orientalis* hybrids

⑳ *Platycodon grandiflorus*

INDIVIDUAL HIGHLIGHT PLANT

Ⓓ *Digitalis ferruginea*

CLIMBER

Trachelospermum jasminoides

POTS

Phyllostachys nigra

HARD LANDSCAPING

It was paramount that in this small urban garden an overall identity was created to bring the disparate spaces together. A simple design with crisp, clean lines, supported by sympathetic contemporary materials, gives the garden clarity and individuality, but at the same time links it to the urban environment. A flow of materials unifies the two outdoor areas. A minimalist approach – echoing the hard, straight lines of the surroundings – is contrasted by a lawn, framed by an area of loose planting, in the rear 'family' garden.

ABOVE *Reminiscent of Japanese moss gardens, the oversized joints between the paving in the enclosed side alley of this property allow plenty of space for* Soleirolia soleirolii *to take hold and green up the shady space.*

PAVING

Low-maintenance paving covers a large area of the garden, creating a simple stylish look with the illusion of expanded garden boundaries. The secret to a successful minimalist–paving layout is in the detail. In large areas, such as this front garden, the quality of the paving and the skill employed in laying it are immediately apparent. A top-end choice, laid perfectly, with well-proportioned slab sizes is essential in creating a cohesive look that brings the spaces together as a whole, and makes the garden appear much larger than its diminutive size.

Here, the diamond-cut Yorkstone was cut into large, rectangular pieces measuring 100 x 40cm (39½ x 15¾in) and 50mm (2in) thick, each piece weighing a considerable amount. It is laid in the front garden in a rectangular asymmetric pattern to give a contemporary and unusual feel. With a main colour of dove grey and swirling brown natural staining, each slab is slightly different from the next. Overall, the effect is a fusion of a natural material with a highly manufactured finish, and so it is perfect for the urban environment. To create a smooth look on an even plane, the paving slabs are laid butt jointed (that is, laid closely together without any mortar joints to distract the eye), and to ensure that there is no movement (sinking areas) all of the paving is laid on a solid concrete foundation. If you're looking to re-create the effect, it is worth employing the services of a professional landscaper.

The front garden is almost entirely covered with Yorkstone, with tall bamboo planted around the edges to provide privacy. This is enhanced by uplighters, which allow the garden to be enjoyed into the evening. The addition of comfortable sofas – ideal for relaxing in and enjoying balmy evenings and conversation, or just for gazing up at passing clouds on sunny afternoons – still allow plenty of room for parties in this space.

In the long side walkway, each slab is painstakingly laid a pace apart (similar to stepping stones), leaving a small gap between and around each stone. Inspired by Japanese moss gardens, planting every crevice with low-growing *Soleirolia soleirolii* (commonly known as Baby's Tears or Mind Your Own Business) makes a deep, maintenance-free green carpet, withstanding both pedestrians and bicycles. The effect is that of paving floating in a sea of green, adding life, vitality and colour to this otherwise shady passageway, and providing the perfect link from the front to the rear garden.

Luckily, in the middle of the passageway, the entrance and step up to the front door have the original tiling, which contrasts wonderfully with the contemporary Yorkstone. The Yorkstone paving extends into the back garden, and is used as a transitional material between the deck and the lawn, and also as access to the storage shed. Here, the paving butts together to make this linking path as understated and easy on the eye as possible.

Do be aware that there are planning regulations governing the laying of paving materials in front gardens. See www.planningportal.gov.uk for the latest advice.

FURNITURE

Furniture and other accessories are key in creating your garden's overall look and should be given consideration at the initial design stage. In the front, adult area, limited colour-coded accessories give a strong architectural look. Huge planters, with a smooth metallic finish, house large olive trees. These have a bold and dominating presence, accentuated by the toning shades in the paving stone and the texture of the woven, architectural furniture – all of which complete the sophisticated look of this garden.

BELOW *Garden furniture adds year-round texture and visual interest, contrasting with the minimalist terrace and limited planting palette of this small space.*

DECKING

Decks are the perfect choice for traversing slopes, uneven ground and varying levels without the need for expensive retaining walls. They are also great at camouflaging ugly, aged patios. In addition, decking can save you money on construction, often negating the need to dig up all but the most decrepit areas of hard landscaping, before covering it with a sheet of weed-proof membrane and then building the deck itself. Hardwood lasts longer than softwood, and, although more expensive, it is best in areas of heavy use or where children play. Here, Balau decking timber is laid on top of a decking frame made of pressure-treated timber – the surface of the deck is level with the bottom sill height of the French windows, leading from the kitchen and family rooms of the house into the garden. This means that the difference in floor height between inside and out is barely noticeable, so the transition from kitchen to alfresco dining area is smooth, without any need to negotiate steps with trays of food or drink.

The steps down from the main deck to the lower area are designed to run across the total rear elevation of the property, with wide treads and low risers; the result is a shallow and gentle level change, which allows for impromptu seating or laid-back lounging, with or without cushions. Lighting is installed in the front rise of the lower step, in order that the steps are flooded with light at ground level, picking up the grain in the timber and the striation of the stone after dark.

Do be aware that there are planning regulations governing the height of decking platforms. See www.planningportal.gov.uk for the latest advice.

BOUNDARIES AND TRELLIS

In the rear garden, and the side walkway, fencing and walling are extended in height to the permitted 2m (6½ft) by using a hardwood horizontal trellis. Sculptural and elegant, this has a more modern architectural look than standard lattice panelling in squares or diamonds. It also offers plenty of privacy. Our trellis is bespoke, but it is relatively simple to construct yourself, using standard roofing batons, and there are off-the-shelf products available, too. See list of suppliers on page 188.

Do be aware that there are planning regulations governing the height of fencing. Usually, it is in respect of fences that are over 1m (3ft) high and situated next to a highway used by vehicles (or the footpath of such a highway); or over 2m (6½ft) high elsewhere, and if your property is listed, adjacent to a listed building, or

ABOVE *Long, generous steps make it easier to move around the garden and can also double up as impromptu seating – perfect for children.*

OPPOSITE *A sunken gravel strip keeps plants and lawn separate while making mowing easier. It also carries the colour of the terracing stone into the wider garden, adding textural interest and making the garden seem larger.*

in a conservation area. See www.planningportal.gov.uk for the latest advice.

LAWN

An emerald swathe of green to lounge on and to tickle toes, this lawn stands out well within the surrounding built-up area, and, although small, is an essential requirement for this urban family garden. As the focal point of the rear garden, and also to make maintenance easier, the square-shaped lawn is edged with the same timber as the deck. Between this edging strip and the paving, large stone cobbles are laid on top of a strip of weed-proof membrane to create visual interest and texture, while allowing a lawn mower to trim right up to the lawn's perimeter, without the need to strim the edges.

PLANTING

Every plant has to work hard to earn its place in the minimalist and small garden. Here, plants were chosen for their architectural qualities and kept to a minimum for maximum impact. The front garden contained only three plants – bamboo, olive trees and rosemary – while in the rear family garden more traditional foliage and flowers were used to soften the hard lines and provide a contrast to the contemporary materials.

FRONT GARDEN

BAMBOO

Infinitely useful in urban spaces, bamboo is the accent plant used in both the rear and front garden. Its tall, elegant, statuesque nature is utilized in the front garden to surround the space, forming a dense hedge and enclosing the garden from the street. *Phyllostachys aurea* is sturdy and strong, and its light green canes, which mature to intense gold, will not make the space too dark. Canes can grow to 5m (16ft), but if this proves to be too tall, simply remove canes from the base of the plant or top the canes that are out of proportion.

Remember that bamboo, contrary to popular belief, is a very hungry, thirsty plant. Regular feeding with fish, blood and bone (or other slow-release fertilizer) is wise – we also fitted a dripper irrigation system to ensure that the plants got as much water as they needed.

ROSEMARY

Although we want the garden to be minimal in both its hard and soft landscaping, we don't want it to be dull. Rosemary is a wonderful, hardworking plant, with hidden, characterful qualities. A fine-leaved upright evergreen rosemary, 'Miss Jessop's Upright' has intensely aromatic grey-green foliage and pretty spikes of small lavender-blue flowers in spring and summer. Excellent for cooking, it has medicinal qualities, too. If you need to treat stomach cramps, colds, stiff muscles, headaches, or even improve your memory, then rosemary's your plant. It is even said to improve scalp conditions and prevent premature baldness. This variety reaches a maximum height of 1m (3ft), so is perfect under the windows in the front garden, where the buzz of the bees it attracts, and the beautiful scent, can be enjoyed inside and out.

OLIVE TREES

The drawing room overlooks the front garden, so some large focal plants were required to give the garden impact and drama. Any plants chosen had to stand out against the green foliage of the bamboo around three sides of the garden. As we had already chosen rosemary to add scent and impact, we decided upon three huge, silvery olive trees to contribute to the Mediterranean flavour. Planted into three oversize pots measuring 70 x 70 x 70cm (27½ x 27½ x 27½in), there is no denying that the three *Olea europaea* were heavy and difficult to plant – definitely a case of more hands making light work. Ensure that you insert any irrigation and lighting cables up through the pot before planting the tree, because taking the plant out of the pot, if these important cables are forgotten, will not be easy.

The olives provide a feathery mass of silvery leaves that are tolerant of hot, dry conditions. In the UK they are often said not to be fully hardy, but as the climate gets milder, the popularity of olive trees continues to grow, particular in the warm shelter of urban gardens.

If you're doubtful of their hardiness, grow olives in pots that can be moved to the shelter of a cool greenhouse over the winter months. If you intend to move pots, always run irrigation and lighting cables up the back of the pots, so that they can be easily unclipped and moved. This is also worth remembering if you are not intending to stay in your property for too long; mature specimen plants, and the pots they are planted in, can be a considerable investment.

OPPOSITE TOP *The fluttering, airy blooms of long-flowering* Gaura lindheimeri *carry the country-cottage planting of the rear garden from spring all the way into autumn. Perfect for the small garden.*

SIDE PASSAGEWAY CARPETING

In order to add greenery to the side passageway we needed to find a low carpeting plant to grow around and between the paving slabs – a plant capable of taking a wide range of abuse from feet, bicycles and buggies. *Soleirolia soleirolii* is the perfect candidate. A maintenance-free ground cover happy in moist, shady areas, *S. soleirolii* will also tolerate sun. While it is a hardy plant, its leaves may be killed by winter frost, but it will recover to grow vigorously in spring. The masses of tiny leaves clothe slender spreading stems that root as they run, forming a dense deep-pile carpet, with a similar appearance to moss.

REAR GARDEN

TRACHELOSPERMUM JASMINOIDES

A woody evergreen climber with dark green leaves turning bronze in winter, Star Jasmine is the perfect urban climber. In the rear garden it will clothe the fencing, which in time will become camouflaged. Clusters of pure white fragrant flowers are produced and the intoxicating perfume is further heightened within the confines of a small urban plot. Grow in well-drained soil in full sun, or partial shade, with protection from cold drying wind.

SHADE PLANTS

Beneath the dusty silver foliage of the existing *Sorbus aria* in the rear garden, a medley of shade-loving border plants provide an informal palette that can be added to with ease. Taller herbaceous perennials, such as *Digitalis ferruginea* and *D. grandiflora*, pierce through the glittering flowerheads of the grass. The foliage of *Deschampsia cespitosa* 'Golden Dew' adds to the ground cover and mixes with the hairy rounded foliage of *Alchemilla mollis* and frothy fern-like foliage of the wine-stained Granny's Bonnet, *Aquilegia* 'Ruby Port'. Hellebores add evergreen interest while the daylily *Hemerocallis* 'Ice Carnival' adds impact and a long flowering period in the sunnier positions of the border.

LEFT *The rear garden planting is in contrast to the more masculine architecture of the front garden. Fences are smothered in evergreen* Trachelospermum jasminoides *behind feminine washes of herbaceous perennials and the shade-tolerant grass* Deschampsia cespitosa *'Golden Dew'.*

METHOD

When carrying out work in a confined space, having a plan of action will avoid costly mistakes. It will allow for staggered deliveries when storage would otherwise be a problem, and, ultimately, it will save your sanity. Here's how.

1 CLEARANCE AND MARK OUT

Before you begin work, draw your garden plan to scale (see page 175) and check that any planning issues have been resolved and agreed. Hire a skip, dress in your old clothes, including steel toecap boots, then reach for the spade and sledgehammer. Removing everything in the garden that you don't require is the very first step in transformation. Perfect for removing pent-up anger, smashing, grabbing and chucking out can be great fun. Remember, if you have to carry debris through the house to reach the skip, or boot of your car, protect your floors first. Once the garden is clear, with your scale garden plan, measure and mark out the garden's components on the ground, using a can of spray line (available from builders' merchants). This life-size ground drawing will allow you to walk along the paths, check the patios for size and make sure that everything is in proportion. It will also help you to finalize what materials you need before you start construction.

2 BOUNDARIES

It's almost always the case that you will start at the edges of your garden and work your way in. Clean down and repoint old brick walls in sections before fixing any trellis to them.

3 SCREENING

For this garden a bespoke trellis was constructed off site, then fixed to 100 x 100mm (4 x 4in) timber posts concreted into the ground at the base of certain sections of the wall, which extended up to the desired height. You can construct a similar trellis yourself using standard roofing batons. Alternatively, there are ready-made off-the-shelf products available too.

ABOVE *Horizontal trellis fixed to the top of fences and walls lends a contemporary feel to urban gardens. It can be made on site, bought in or commissioned.*

4 LIGHTING AND IRRIGATION

If you choose to install lighting, it's always best to call upon the services of a qualified electrician to carry out the 'first fix'; if you are employing a landscape contractor to build your garden then they can organize this for you. Lay electric cables, conduit pipes and irrigation hardware in position before your paving and decks are laid.

5 DECKING

Start by building your timber frame. For this garden a timber frame was built over the existing stone terrace, with support boards fixed to the boundary walls and to posts concreted into position at intervals (see page 164 for more details on deck construction). Smooth Balau boards are fitted to the frame, using stainless-steel decking screws. After a final sand, oil the deck to maintain its rich colour.

6 PAVING

Working your way down the side passageway into the front garden, the paving is the last hard landscaping job to carry out. Checking and rechecking your lines is of paramount importance. If the lines of your house are not entirely square, a certain amount of tweaking and laying by eye will be necessary to get the look just so. Slabs are extremely heavy, and, as planting is required between each slab in the passageway, you may want to employ the services of a professional landscape contractor for this. Leave the paving to settle for a few days before finishing the lighting, painting rendered walls, backfilling the beds and containers then digging in compost to the flower beds in preparation for planting. (See page 163 for more details on how to lay paving.)

7 PLANTING

The impact of bringing a few plants into an empty space always amazes me. The addition of a living thing adds magic to the newly landscaped space. If you can afford to, ensure that all your plants arrive at the same time so you can place them in the beds, change your mind and reshuffle them around (it'll happen, believe me!), before finally planting into well-prepared soil with added compost and feed. Always finish your planting with a mulch (bark chip is perfect) to feed the soil, retain moisture, keep down weeds and give a polished professional finish. (See page 176 for more details on preparing borders and containers for plants.)

RIGHT *The gnarled stems and shimmering foliage of mature olives become living sculpture.*

BELOW *Used en masse, the smallest of plants can make a big impact, especially when contrasted with hard materials.*

MAINTENANCE

JANUARY

Winter gales can blow leaves from surrounding gardens into yours. Keep your borders free from leaves, which can cause plant crowns to rot if they accumulate.

Order any seeds and summer flowering bulbs you might like to add to your borders or pots.

FEBRUARY

Snowfall can weigh heavily on woody plants, even causing branches to break. After very heavy snowfall, clear snow from your trees, shrubs and climbers, if you can bear to!

If a friend has snowdrops in their garden, now's the time to split them – if there are any spare plant them in your garden!

MARCH

As the longer days of spring arrive, top up the layer of bark-chip mulch in your borders.

Lift and divide overgrown clumps of grasses, replanting what you need and potting up excess plants to give away to friends.

APRIL

Annual weeds will start to pop up here and there; your raised beds should make weeding easy.

MAY

Now's your last chance to trim back dead growth on herbaceous perennials before they start actively growing.

If you haven't done so already, feed all your border plants with a slow-release fertilizer such as fish, blood and bone.

JUNE

Plant herbs in the garden close to the house so that they are easily harvested for cooking.

JULY

Keep your borders and pots watered, looking out for pests and diseases as you go.

Plant autumn-flowering bulbs such as Colchicum and autumn flowering crocus.

AUGUST

Give all your pots and containers a good feed with a liquid fertilizer.

SEPTEMBER

It's the start of the planting season, and you could add some additional climbers to your garden's boundary (perhaps roses in the rear garden) or fill any gaps in your borders.

OCTOBER

Plant lily, tulip and allium bulbs to add impact to your borders next year.

NOVEMBER

Tidy up the garden for winter, removing any collapsed or ugly dead flowerheads.

DECEMBER

Feed the birds in this cold weather, ensuring that they have a supply of fresh, unfrozen water.

Shady terraces are prone to algae; if yours is looking a little green, or dirty, hire a pressure washer and clean it now.

EDIBLE GARDEN

PLANNING THE GARDEN

More and more garden owners want to grow their own vegetables. An urban back yard or the tiniest scrap of land can be turned into a productive space, filled with homegrown fruit and vegetables. And with an increasing desire to eat healthily, there's never been a better time to grow your own. Going organic allows you to avoid the inflated supermarket costs of fruit and veg that has travelled thousands of miles to reach your plate. Starting your home allotment is easier than you think, and, if the going gets tough, always remember: fresh is best!

Growing fruit and vegetables effectively is basically no different from growing ornamental plants successfully. Take care of them and they'll take care of you. Start with good plants or seeds, give them what they want – food, water and light – and they'll do the work for you.

DESIGN ELEMENTS

Urban gardens are often squeezed into the most awkward of spaces, resulting in strange shapes that challenge designers, let alone garden owners. But what is often considered a negative can become a positive. An interesting shape can result in a stimulating, striking space to spend time in – as long as it has been carefully considered in advance and a good design solution has been implemented.

In this L-shaped plot two gardens in one have been created. The first is a contemporary space that blurs the interior/exterior divide, extending the living space, from kitchen-diner to terrace, into an outdoor room. As the owner is a chef, the second space is a kitchen/vegetable garden, or potager, which, although out of view, has key landscaping features linking the spaces together. Some plants have also been chosen to provide cut flowers for the table. As the garden is east facing, the area outside the kitchen door loses the sun as the day progresses. However, even very small gardens can accommodate various seating areas, allowing you to follow the sun's progress and offering alternative positions from which to admire the views.

A secondary terrace has been built in a corner of the garden, nestled behind tall layers of planting, to make the most of evening light. A small deck beside the

ABOVE *Even if your space is tiny, always include plenty of opportunities to sit, relax and admire the view.*

potting shed in the vegetable garden provides another perch to rest on between gardening jobs.

The client here was interested in using unusual garden materials and design treatments. Creating an area for storage was also a requirement, and, rather than installing a standard garden shed, the idea was to investigate more interesting structures.

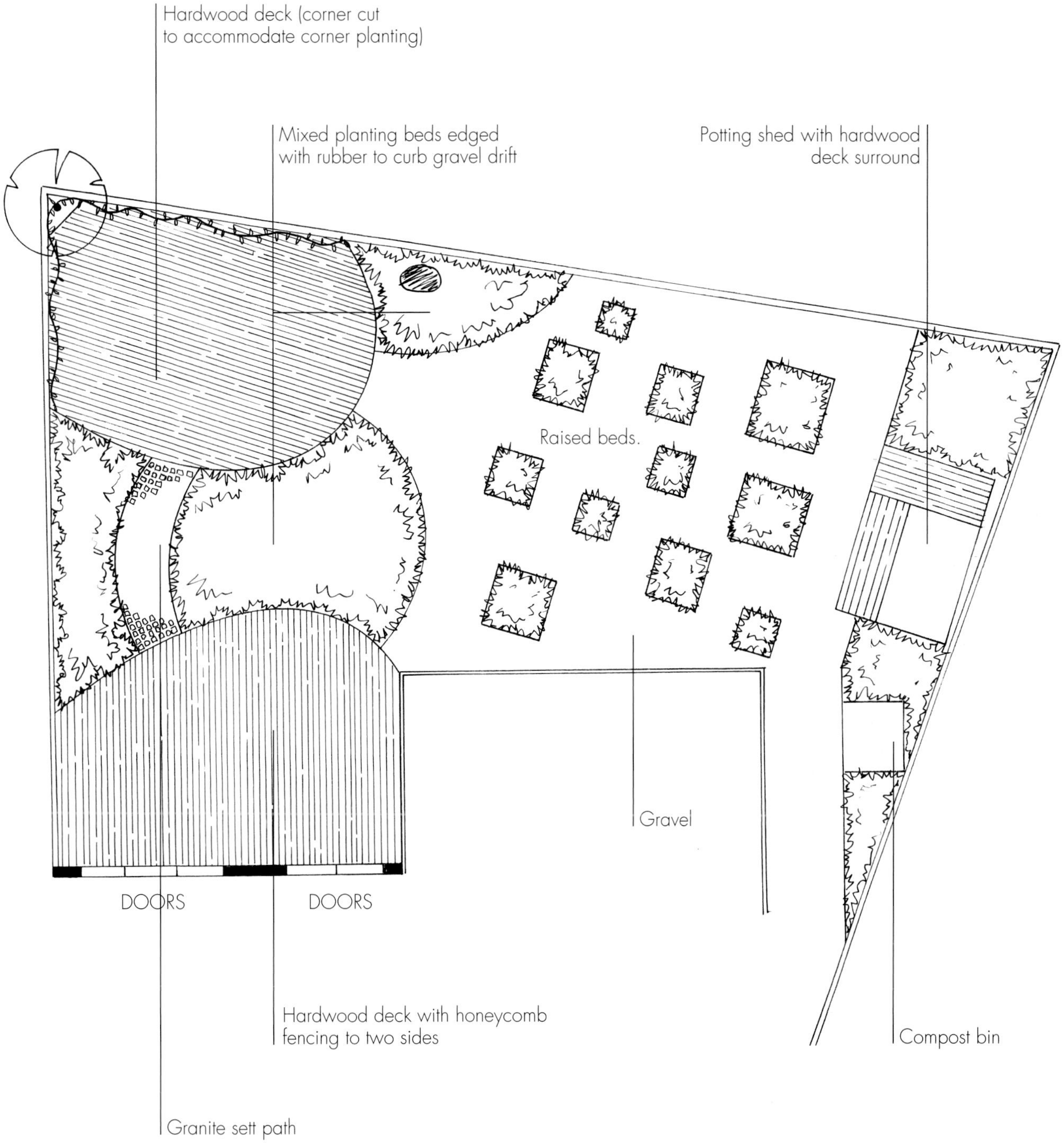

Hardwood deck (corner cut
to accommodate corner planting)

Mixed planting beds edged
with rubber to curb gravel drift

Potting shed with hardwood
deck surround

Raised beds.

Gravel

DOORS   DOORS

Hardwood deck with honeycomb
fencing to two sides

Granite sett path

Compost bin

WHAT YOU WILL NEED

HARD LANDSCAPING

Skip

Concrete mixer

DECKING

100 x 100mm (4 x 4in) pressure-treated timber posts for decking frame

100 x 50mm (4 x 2in) pressure-treated timber joists

90mm (3½in) decking frame screws

145 x 20mm (5¾ x ¾in) smooth Balau hardwood decking boards

60mm (2⅛in) decking screws – 28 screws per square metre

Concrete to support frame posts: ballast and ordinary Portland cement (5:1 ratio) plus water

FENCING

Fence panels for the boundary and for any screening

Treated (tanalised) roofing panels

75 x 75mm x 2.4m (3 x 3in x 8ft) timber fence posts

Gravel boards

Postfix ready-mix concrete

Wood screws

Fence clips

EDGING FOR BORDERS

Flexible metal border edging

RAISED VEGETABLE BOXES

100 x 100mm (4 x 4in) posts concreted into the ground

Postfix ready-mix concrete (20kg bags) to secure vertical support posts. One bag will fill a 30 x 30 x 30cm (12 x 12 x 12in) hole. Use 40kg of concrete per post to ensure it remains stable.

145 x 32mm (5¾ x 1¼in) smooth Balau decking boards

60mm (2⅛in) Spax wood screws to fix decking to joist framework – 28 screws per metre

GRAVEL PATH IN VEGETABLE GARDEN

MOT type 1 scalpings

Basalt stone chippings 20–40mm (¾–1½in) in size

LIGHTING

Adjustable spotlights in powder-coated finish

Deck lights

Cables, clips and other accessories

Transformers

Junction boxes

Remote control

NB You will need to measure your garden carefully in order to establish the quantities required to suit your particular space. All lighting should be installed by a qualified electrician.

PLANTING

Compost

Mulch

Gravel for drainage

Slow-release fertilizer

MAIN CENTRAL BED

Acanthus spinosus

Acer palmatum dissectum 'Atropurpureum'

Agapanthus 'White Heaven'

Artichoke variety

Astrantia major 'Rubra'

Beta vulgaris 'Ruby Red'

Cabbage varieties

Climbing beans

Echinops ritro 'Veitch's Blue'

Eryngium bourgatii

Eryngium planum 'Blaukappe'

Eunonymus fortunei 'Emerald 'n' Gold'

Fatsia japonica

Headbourne hybrids

Helenium 'Sahin's Early Flowerer'

Heuchera 'Crème Brûlée'

Hosta fortunei 'Aureomarginata'

Hosta 'Patriot'

Leucanthemum 'Highland White Dream'

Ligularia dentata 'Desdemona'

Nicotiana sylvestris

Phormium 'Flamingo'

Sweetcorn 'Swift'

Swiss chard 'Bright Lights'

Tiarella cordifolia

Tomato 'Totem'

Verbena bonariensis

VEGETABLE GARDEN

Allium schoenoprasum

American Landcress

Batavia salad

Blueberry 'Northsky'

Chilli 'Apache'

Climbing French beans

Foeniculum vulgare

Lathyrus odoratus sp.

Laurus nobilis (topiary pyramid)

Lavandula stoechas

Mustard 'Green Frills'

Perpetual Spinach

Potato 'Charlotte'

Potato 'Duke of York'

Rhubarb 'Glaskins Perpetual'

Rosmarinus officinalis

Salvia officinalis 'Tricolor'

Thymus vulgaris

Tomato 'Beefsteak'

Tomato 'Italian Plum'

Tomato 'Sungold'

TREE

Robinia pseudoacacia 'Frisia'

BENEATH TREE

Brunnera macrophylla 'Jack Frost'

Digitalis 'Camelot White'

Polystichum setiferum

Tropaeolum majus 'Jewel Mixed'

x *Fatshedera lizei*

BOUNDARY NEAR PATH

Cabbage varieties

Phyllostachys aurea

CLIMBERS

Parthenocissus quinquefolia

PLANTS IN POTS

Agapanthus 'Blue Prince'

Hosta 'Sum and Substance'

Zantedeschia aethiopica 'Crowborough'

NB Plants are usually grouped in numbers of 3, 5 and 7, but the numbers you choose should be determined by the size of your garden.

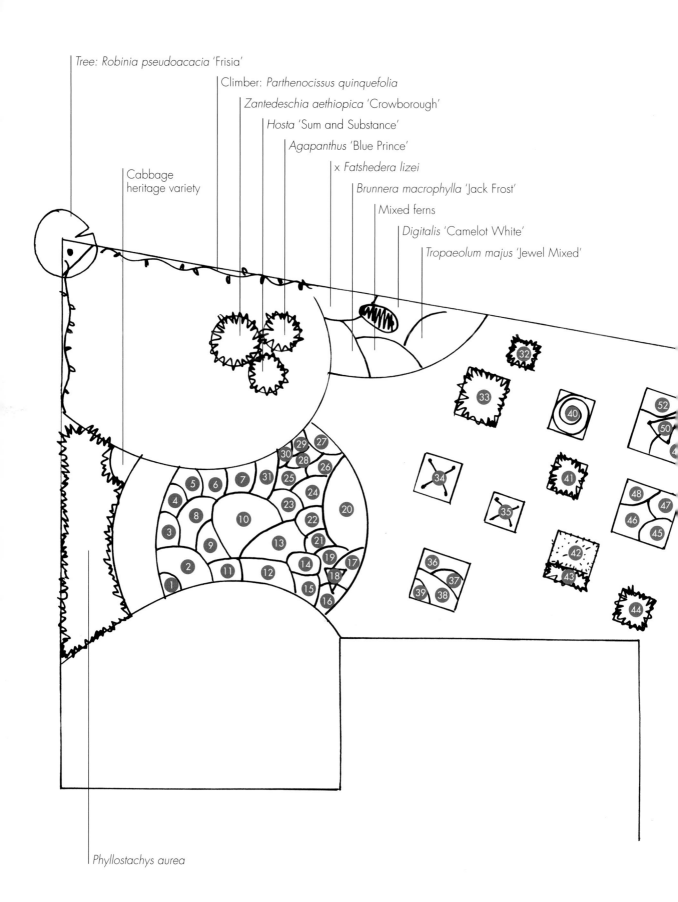

Tree: *Robinia pseudoacacia* 'Frisia'

Climber: *Parthenocissus quinquefolia*

Zantedeschia aethiopica 'Crowborough'

Hosta 'Sum and Substance'

Agapanthus 'Blue Prince'

x *Fatshedera lizei*

Brunnera macrophylla 'Jack Frost'

Mixed ferns

Digitalis 'Camelot White'

Tropaeolum majus 'Jewel Mixed'

Cabbage
heritage variety

Phyllostachys aurea

PLANTING PLAN

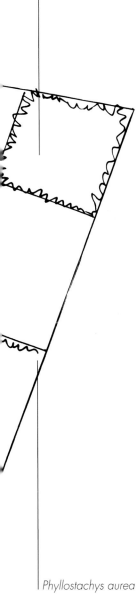

Phyllostachys aurea

Phyllostachys aurea

MAIN BED

1. Cabbage heritage variety
2. *Fatsia japonica*
3. Swiss chard 'Bright Lights'
4. Tomato 'Totem'
5. *Phormium* 'Flamingo'
6. *Beta vulgaris* 'Ruby Red'
7. *Echinops ritro* 'Veitch's Blue'
8. *Acer palmatum dissectum* 'Atropurpureum'
9. *Eryngium bourgatii*
10. *Leucanthemum* 'Highland White Dream'
11. *Hosta* 'Patriot'
12. *Agapanthus* 'White Heaven'
13. *Eryngium planum* 'Blaukappe'
14. *Eunonymus fortunei* 'Emerald 'n' Gold'
15. Tomato 'Totem'
16. Cabbage heritage variety
17. *Tiarella cordifolia*
18. Climbing beans
19. Artichoke variety
20. *Helenium* 'Sahin's Early Flowerer'
21. *Agapanthus* 'White Heaven'
22. *Nicotiana sylvestris*
23. Sweetcorn 'Swift'
24. *Phormium* 'Flamingo'
25. *Ligularia dentata* 'Desdemona'
26. *Astrantia major* 'Rubra'
27. Cabbage heritage variety
28. *Heuchera* 'Crème Brûlée'
29. *Hosta fortunei* 'Aureomarginata'
30. *Astrantia major* 'Rubra'
31. *Acanthus spinosus*

Main bed dotted through with *Verbena bonariensis*

RAISED BEDS

32. Mint varieties
33. Potato 'Duke of York' and 'Charlotte'
34. *Lathyrus odoratus* sp.
35. Climbing French beans
36. *Salvia officinalis* 'Tricolor'
37. *Allium schoenoprasum*
38. *Foeniculum vulgare*
39. *Thymus* species
40. *Laurus nobilis* (topiary pyramid)
41. *Lavandula stoechas*
42. Tomato 'Beefsteak', 'Sungold' or 'Italian Plum'
43. Perpetual Spinach
44. *Rosmarinus officinalis*
45. Blueberry 'Northsky'
46. Tomato 'Sungold' or 'Italian Plum'
47. Rhubarb 'Glaskins Perpetual'
48. Chilli 'Apache'
49. Batavia salad
50. Climbing French beans
51. Mixed salad
52. American Landcress and Mustard 'Green Frills'

HARD LANDSCAPING

DECKING

Decks provide a quick and cost-effective way to cover large areas. They avoid the work and expense involved in laying foundations to a level base, which is required with paving. Here, a supporting joist framework was built in sections to accommodate the majority of the decked surface area. A separate frame fixed to this supported the curve at the front leading edge of both decked areas. Laying the boards at a slanting angle creates interest and leads the eye out into the garden.

GRAVEL

Gravel is easy to lay, cost effective, low maintenance and, not least, porous. It is perfect in the vegetable garden, where compost is often scattered around. Here, where raised beds in the form of boxes punctuate the space, it would be difficult to lay paving, as it would require a great deal of cutting. Because of gravel's small size, it easily flows around awkward corners, becoming a wash of colour underfoot. An occasional rake and hose down will quickly clean the area up if required. Gravel is available in a huge range of colours and in varying sizes to suit your garden style. Here, dense grey-coloured stones have been used, which echo the city surroundings and give a softer-looking surface. Be careful to make sure that gravel is contained in areas where it meets grass or borders as it can migrate.

SETT PATH

An increasing range of natural stone and man-made setts in varying textures and colours has recently become available. The small size of setts allows them to be laid easily in a curve. Here, granite setts are used as an informal sweeping path through lush, verdant planting, linking one seating area to another. Keeping the path narrow adds to the feeling of adventure as you wade through the densely planted border.

RAISED VEGETABLE BEDS

Raising the level of your crops to a more manageable height is a boon in a potager garden. Raised beds can be filled with high-quality soil and it's easy to add compost or other organic matter. Long-rooted plants, such as carrots, do especially well in this environment. Plants in raised beds get more sun and air circulation and they can make better use of water. You can often plant earlier and harvest later, because the beds warm up early in the spring and stay warm later in the autumn. Raised beds also make ideal places to grow plants that can be invasive in a regular garden, such as mint and horseradish. But, for many gardeners, easy access is the main advantage. A raised bed may put an end to the aches and pains, such as a bad back and sore knees, that you get from gardening. They are also excellent for people in wheelchairs.

Fill the frame with a lightweight soil mix (see page 173) and add a generous amount of compost. Avoid using soil straight from the garden. It's usually too heavy and doesn't allow for proper drainage. A well-constructed raised bed should last for years, and soil fertility can be maintained by adding organic matter.

Vegetable gardening in raised beds is similar to growing plants in containers, but on a larger scale. The main difference is that the bottom of a raised bed is left open, so plant roots can grow deeper into the existing ground. A raised bed is ideal if you have poor, sandy, rocky or wet soil.

In this garden the beds vary in height and size, while the planting boxes have been spaced out enough to allow a wheelbarrow to pass through. The maximum width of each bed should be about 1.2m (4ft), allowing easy access from the sides when you are planting, weeding and cropping. Although they vary in size, all of the boxes are square in order to create a cohesive look, but they could be any shape you like.

FENCING

Fencing often marks the boundary of your garden and usually forms the backdrop to any scheme. If you're looking for fencing that is slightly more interesting than the ubiquitous larch lap panelled fence, then the market has opened up in recent years with some great 'off the peg' alternatives. In this garden, 'hit and miss' panels, formed from two layers of offset horizontal boards (one at the front and one at the back) have been used for cost

ABOVE *Sheds can dominate the view in a small garden. Make sure that yours deserves visual prominence.*

effectiveness and to give a clean, contemporary look. Hit and miss panels are perfect for windy locations because the wind can still pass through the panels. (A more solid barrier may result in panels blowing down on a particularly windy day, or could even encourage the wind to eddy over the fence, building in force as it does so and doing more damage where it eventually comes down to ground level.) The top of the fence has horizontal roofing batons fixed to the fence supports to give a more decorative finish.

In the seating area close to the house, a different mood has been created with the use of recycled honeycomb fence panels. These undulating honeycomb structures were commissioned by a designer in order to add a real talking point in the garden. An everyday functional object has become a sculpture in its own right, constantly changing as sunlight passes across the surface, and coming into its own when lit at night. This sculptural slant on practical landscaping is further highlighted by the bespoke potting shed in the potager section of the garden.

When commissioning bespoke items, always be completely clear about your expectations. Full working drawings will ensure that your ideas are successfully interpreted and will allow the designer to give accurate costings, delivery dates and constructional advice. Make sure that everything is agreed in writing, including terms and conditions, from the moment of commission.

POTTING SHED

When you're growing vegetables, some kind of storage for tools, pots, propagating trays and shelter to bring on seedlings is absolutely essential. However, if you're looking for something a little more eye-catching and architectural than the average garden shed, then some detective work is required. The shed in this garden was initially designed as a container in which to transport the honeycomb fence panels. Part of it was recycled (as was the fencing) and used to form the front panel of the potting shed, allowing a space for shelter, storage and to raise plants.

LIGHTING

Even in the city, with lots of surrounding ambient lighting, garden lights will extend the hours spent outside long into the evening. Adjustable spike lights within the borders highlight specimen plants after dark and can be moved and adjusted depending on which plants are looking their best. The honeycomb fence and potting shed have lighting of their own, with lights incorporated in the decking boards at the base of the panels in order to uplight them to extra special effect at night.

BELOW *Using the same timber for the raised planters and the decking ensures visual links to pull the garden together.*

PLANTING

VEGETABLES IN THE MIXED BORDER

For the determined vegetable gardener, limited space need not be an issue. Many vegetables are very beautiful in their own right and work perfectly within a mixed border; good soil, plenty of sunshine, water and a good eye are all that's needed. Combine vegetables with attractive hardy perennials and grow specimen plants in pots. A small garden can be extremely lush and verdant when every scrap of space is used to create a productive garden for flowers and fodder too!

As many vegetables are extremely decorative, planting

BELOW *Some vegetables, such as this artichoke, are as beautiful as many perennials and can certainly hold their own in the mixed border.*

them in flower borders can give surprising, and often sensational results. Historically, in the cottage garden, vegetables were grown with flowers as a necessity, and a recent upsurge of interest in growing your own has seen a revival in this planting style. Globe artichokes are an obvious choice for a mixed border, where its ornamental cousin *Cynara cardunculus* is often grown. In this culinary-inspired, small space vegetable garden, it makes much more sense to grow an artichoke you can eat, especially when the ground it takes up is minimal compared to the impact it delivers with its vertical height. It is the base of the mature flower bud that you eat. Good edible varieties of artichoke include the popular 'Green Globe', as well as the purple-headed '*Violetta di Chioggia*' and '*Fiesole*'. Globe artichokes are perennial vegetables, producing crops year after year and giving even better yields with the occasional addition of compost and the odd feed. Climbing beans are another space-saving flower border addition, as they climb up rather than out, their delicate flowers giving way to a hanging larder of edible fruit. Finally, choose some more buxom foliage plants to add a contrast to more delicate herbaceous perennials – in this garden cabbages have been used to great architectural effect.

VEGETABLE GARDENING IN RAISED BEDS

As an accomplished cook, the owner of this garden wanted an attractive, ornamental kitchen garden/potager where she could conveniently grow her favourite vegetables and herbs. A raised-bed vegetable garden was the perfect solution. The beds provide ideal conditions for growing a host of plants; flat green bean pods swell and ripen against sweet peas grown for the table, which, at the same time, impart their delicious scent. Herbs such as rosemary, thyme, chives and sage overflow from their boxes, releasing their scent and tempting anyone who brushes against them into picking, smelling or tasting them. Spinach and potatoes thrive amidst more permanent plantings of rhubarb, as do salad crops. Soil can be changed in order to accommodate a plant's needs – ericaceous compost has been added to one of the boxes in order to ensure a crop of plump, delicious, but acid-loving blueberries.

ABOVE *In a small garden, grow vegetables that are hard to get hold of, expensive to buy, or that you simply love. All add texture, colour and form to mixed plantings.*

New crops can be planted once a crop has 'gone over' (finished producing/flowering); peas, carrots, squash, sweetcorn, cucumbers and so forth can all be planted late in the season for harvesting later in the year.

PLANTS IN POTS

Pots play an important part in the small garden, allowing you to grow a range of plants that can be changed at whim, and set against a backdrop of more permanent plantings. They should be as large as possible to create impact, and, practically speaking, the bigger the pot, the less watering is required. Containers work best when planters of the same material, or similar design, are grouped together; if you have a medley of terracotta, wood and plastic pots, painting them all the same colour

can create a more cohesive look. Here, oversized pots have been used to great effect, taking on the role of architectural focal point at the rear of the garden. Although different sizes, they are made from the same material and give impact and height when set against the garden fence at the back of the secondary seating area. Rather than mixing plant varieties, cramming pots with one species of plants adds further impact. Here, a mass of *Zantedeschia aethiopica* and *Agapanthus* 'Blue Prince', both of which seem to perform best when their roots are slightly pot bound, are highlighted when elevated and framed in a stunning pot. And the voluptuous *Hosta* 'Sum and Substance' is kept away from all but the most adventurous of slugs, which at ground level would certainly decimate the glorious large leaves for which it is known and loved.

PLANTING BENEATH TREES

Trees cast shade and sap the moisture in the soil, so planting beneath them is regarded as one of the most difficult situations for growing plants. However, there are a few plants that will grow in these conditions. They can be helped along if you improve the soil by adding compost and a mulch around your plants and remember to water them regularly. Plant ideas include *Digitalis*, *Euphorbia amygdaloides* var. *robbiae*, *Epimedium*, *Alchemilla mollis*, *Geranium macrorrhizum* and, as used in this garden, *Brunnera macrophylla* 'Jack Frost', *Digitalis* 'Camelot White', *Tropaeolum majus* (nasturtium), *Polystichum setiferum* and x *Fatshedera lizei*.

BELOW *Cabbage at the front of a mixed border saves space, softens the decking and looks as architectural as many purely ornamental plants.*

METHOD

1 CLEARANCE AND MARK OUT

Remove everything that you don't want to keep, including any remaining panels of decrepit fencing. Usually, this will involve negotiations with your neighbours to establish which boundary fencing belongs to them, whether they are willing to contribute to the new fencing, and what to use as a replacement. If you are unsure as to which boundaries are yours, this is usually marked upon the deeds of your house. Mark out with spray line (available from builders' merchants) the layout of your new garden, including the curve of the proposed deck(s). This is best done by placing a peg in the ground, then, using a piece of string stretched from the peg, mark out the shape or circle that you propose with canes. Next, spray line the edge of the shape.

2 FENCING

All fence posts should be concreted into the ground and left slightly longer than the fence panels, so as to accommodate the horizontal trellis. Fix the fence panels to the posts, checking then rechecking that they are level as you go. Attach the timber roofing batons to the extended fence posts with screws, adding intermediate support panels where necessary. Begin with the bottom horizontal and work upwards.

3 ELECTRICS

Lay electric cables to accommodate a low-voltage lighting system. Do this before the decking boards are laid over the frame and make sure that cables go under any hard landscaping. It is advisable to use a professional when setting up an outdoor electrical system.

4 DECKING

Build timber frames for decking terraces. These are held in position by upright support posts that you will need to concrete into the ground at intervals. Fix the decking boards to the posts, overrunning at the edges, before marking out then cutting the curves using a jigsaw. Provide extra support beneath the curve where necessary.

ABOVE *Gravel is a wonderfully low-maintenance surface in the vegetable garden, as spills of soil or compost are easily hosed away. The large-gauge stone used here is weighty, which stops the gravel from migrating around the garden with your wheelbarrow.*

5 SETT PATH

Pushing them directly into a bed of concrete, lay the setts in a curve to link the two decks.

6 FLEXIBLE METAL EDGING BETWEEN GRAVEL AND BORDERS

It is important to provide an edging between the flowerbed and the gravel to keep both areas crisp and to ensure that they don't migrate into one another. Mark out the position of the edgings with a spade. Place your edging into position. Then, using a rubber mallet, drive the edging into the ground, interlocking pieces as you go and bending it where appropriate to create a curve. Metal spikes at the bottom of each edging strip ensure a good firm finish. This kind of edging is not only very strong, but also very thin and once *in situ* (when flush with the finished soil and gravel level) is almost invisible to the eye.

7 POTTING SHED

Once the main garden area is completed, work can start on the vegetable garden and its main structure: the potting shed. Firstly, lay a concrete foundation for the shed and allow it to set. Generally, building a garden shed is not too difficult as the four side panels and roof are ready made, but, as this shed was bespoke, specialist carpenters were employed to carry out the works.

8 RAISED VEGETABLE GARDEN BOXES

Mark out where you want to position the boxes. Concrete four posts into the ground for each box. Build the boxes around the posts, using decking boards to give continuity in materials and a visual link through the garden.

9 GRAVEL

Lay a subbase of MOT type 1 scalpings around the boxes in the vegetable garden up to the metal edging strip. Compact this with a vibrating plate compacter (available to hire from most good hire shops) to provide a good base. This ensures that once the gravel is laid the area is easy to walk on, avoiding the 'beach' feeling so often associated with gravel in gardens.

10 BORDER AND VEGETABLE-BOX SOIL PREPARATION

Dig over all the border and beds and add compost and slow-release fertilizer to all areas. It is advisable to put some gravel in the vegetable beds for drainage before adding the compost. You can fill some boxes with ericaceous compost to accommodate acid-loving plants.

11 PLANTING

Lay out your plants where you want to position them before planting. The vegetable garden beds will evolve once vegetable seeds have been cultivated (or young plants bought) and planted out at the right time.

12 FINAL ELECTRICS AND MULCH

Finally, complete the electrics. Do this before adding mulch to all planted borders to keep the weeds down, retain moisture in the ground, feed the soil and give a crisp, professional finish.

BELOW *A simple stone sett path allows you to walk between the two decks through a jungle of ornamental and edible plants.*

MAINTENANCE

JANUARY

Encourage early stems of rhubarb by covering them with a large pot to exclude any light.

Clear spent vegetable crops from the garden.

Sow broad beans, lettuces, cabbages, cauliflowers, radishes, carrots, spinach, spring onions, tomatoes and turnips in pots on the windowsill ready for planting out later.

Save egg boxes, ready for chitting seed potatoes in February.

Sow sweet peas in a heated propagator in toilet-roll tubes filled with compost.

FEBRUARY

Plant out lettuces, cabbages, cauliflowers, radishes, carrots, spinach, spring onions and turnips sown in pots in January.

Chit potato tubers to promote strong and vigorous plants. They are ready to plant into the garden when shoots are 2.5 cm (1 in) long.

Cut back perennials that are looking past their best.

Plant up pots with lily bulbs.

Feed your blueberry bush, if you have one.

MARCH

Sow broad beans, carrots, parsnips, beetroot, salad, radishes, peas and spinach directly outside.

Prune your blueberries by removing old and weak branches.

Remove the pot from your rhubarb crowns and allow them to grow naturally.

Plant shallots, onions and garlic sets.

Pot up tomato seedlings.

Plant summer flowering bulbs into the mixed flower border.

Plant out your potatoes, carefully earthing up shoots with soil every time they appear until the shoots are just buried.

APRIL

Plant clematis, honeysuckle and wisteria to cover your boundary fence.

Sow herbs on the windowsill.

Sow beetroots, carrots, Swiss chards, summer cauliflowers, kohlrabi, lettuces, leeks, radishes, turnips, peas and perpetual spinach into well-prepared soil.

Feed your rhubarb.

MAY

Sow French and runner beans, squashes, cucumbers, pumpkins, cauliflowers, purple sprouting broccoli, sweetcorn and young artichoke and tomato plants.

Plant out strawberry and tomato plants.

Plant out your sweet peas into the garden below a structure of canes.

Put supports in the ground for herbaceous perennials before they begin growing.

JUNE

Begin harvesting vegetables.

Continue sowing salad, beetroots and radishes to ensure crops throughout the season.

Begin harvesting early potatoes.

Sow courgettes, marrows, sweetcorn and pumpkins outside.

Plant out vegetables sown indoors earlier in the year.

Sow basil and coriander every other week until the end of June.

Keep on top of weeds.

Tie your sweet peas to their supports.

Keep pots well watered.

JULY

Pick courgettes before they become marrows and pick beans and peas regularly.

Sow spring cabbage, turnips, chicory, fennel and autumn and winter salads.

Continue to keep on top of weeds.

Regularly deadhead the flower garden.

Plant autumn flowering bulbs such as autumn crocus, Colchicums and Nerines.

AUGUST

Harvest sweetcorn as it ripens. Regularly harvest and crop vegetables before they become stringy or tough.

Keep tomatoes well watered.

SEPTEMBER

Dig up and store potatoes in paper bags.

Keep harvesting vegetables as they ripen.

Begin lifting and dividing overgrown clumps of perennials.

OCTOBER

Lift and divide your rhubarb if it's starting to overtake the planting box.

Clear spent pea and bean plants, cutting off top growth and digging roots into the soil — they will add nitrogen to the earth as they rot down.

Lift and divide herbs, bringing small pots into the kitchen to overwinter.

NOVEMBER

Lift and store carrots, beetroots and turnips.

Order seed catalogues.

Keep harvesting vegetables as they mature.

Plant garlic cloves into free-draining raised beds.

Continue cutting back faded perennials, leaving some seedheads to give winter interest.

DECEMBER

Plant fruit trees on dwarf rootstock and fruit bushes.

Clear spent vegetables from the plots and cover empty boxes with black polythene to make them easier to work in spring.

ROMANTIC FRONT GARDEN

PLANNING THE GARDEN

Lying just beyond the garden gate, this inviting romantic garden provides an escape from the city. Set against the French-inspired architecture of the house, the garden incorporates schemes from rural France, which fit compactly into the small urban space. It was imperative to use classic design in this front garden so that the space would not date. This was best achieved by using traditional materials, such as Yorkstone, alongside scented billowing plants and a tiered succession of blooms around the lawn. The different elements work together well to provide an oasis of calm. A feeling of tranquility and space is achieved by keeping the layout simple.

DESIGN ELEMENTS

Living in the centre of the city, but with their hearts firmly in the country, the owners wanted a peaceful garden to relax in and enjoy. Inspired by French architecture, they renovated their property using reclaimed or imported materials to create a timelessly elegant house. The front of the house, with its elegant and imposing front door, called for a garden design that would make the most of the south-facing aspect, give a welcoming appearance to visitors and include space for off-street parking.

BELOW *Bold and yet romantic: topiary 'lollipops', with lavender spread at their feet, add visual weight to the front garden path and are extremely elegant.*

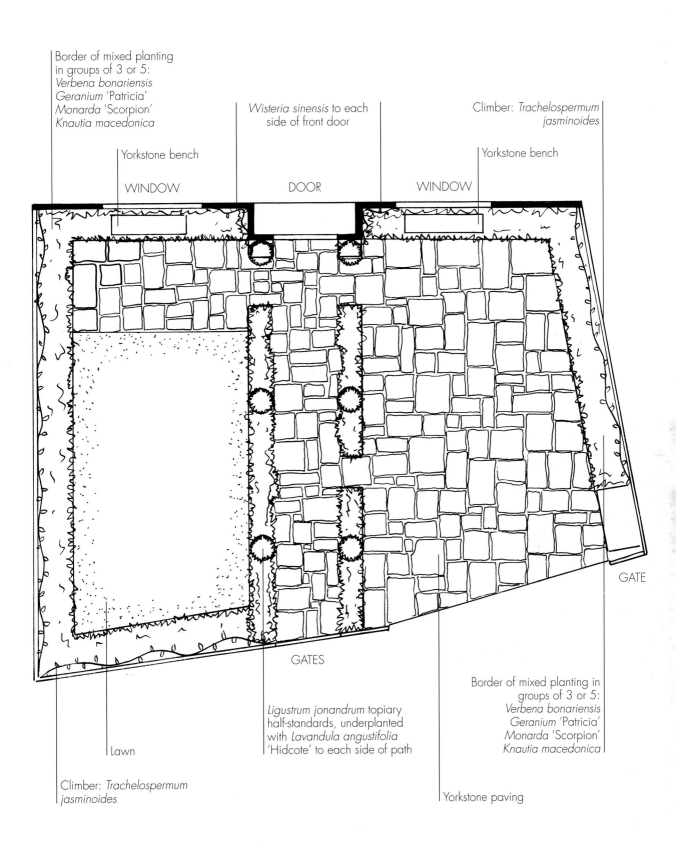

Border of mixed planting
in groups of 3 or 5:
Verbena bonariensis
Geranium 'Patricia'
Monarda 'Scorpion'
Knautia macedonica

Wisteria sinensis to each
side of front door

Climber: *Trachelospermum
jasminoides*

Yorkstone bench

Yorkstone bench

WINDOW

DOOR

WINDOW

Lawn

Climber: *Trachelospermum
jasminoides*

GATES

Ligustrum jonandrum topiary
half-standards, underplanted
with *Lavandula angustifolia*
'Hidcote' to each side of path

Border of mixed planting in
groups of 3 or 5:
Verbena bonariensis
Geranium 'Patricia'
Monarda 'Scorpion'
Knautia macedonica

Yorkstone paving

GATE

WHAT YOU WILL NEED

HARD LANDSCAPING

Skip

Concrete mixer

PAVING:

100mm (4in) depth of MOT type 1 scalpings for foundations

Sharp sand and cement for bedding paving and brick edging (5:1 ratio)

Reclaimed Yorkstone

Soft sand and cement mix (4:1 ratio) for pointing paving

Reclaimed Yorkstone for seating

NB Measure your garden carefully, in order to establish the quantities required to suit your space.

PLANTING

Compost

Slow-release plant food

Bark-chip mulch

Grade 1 lawn

PLANTS

Geranium 'Patricia'

Knautia macedonica

Lavandula angustifolia 'Hidcote'

Ligustrum jonandrum topiary lollipops

Monarda 'Scorpion'

Trachelospermum jasminoides

Verbena bonariensis

Wisteria sinensis

NB Plants are usually grouped in numbers of 3, 5 and 7, but the numbers you choose should be determined by the size of your garden.

RIGHT *A brick wall is a wonderful asset in any garden, the warmth radiating from the walls intensifying and enclosing the scented plants, such as climbing* Trachelospermum jasminoides *and the lavender hedge seen in this front garden.*

HARD LANDSCAPING

PAVING

To create a cohesive look, Yorkstone has been used to form both the paths and the driveway. This natural sandstone with its subtle variation of colour and surface texture is a classic garden paving material. Although these days reclaimed stone is certainly not a cheaper option than newly sawn, in the smaller garden it's worth considering as an investment. Reclaimed stones instantly provide a feeling of age and permanence. In this garden large pieces have been expressly sought out to give gravitas and a sense of grandeur to the space.

By using one paving material throughout the garden, the driveway is integrated and does not dominate the space – it is still visually appealing whether a car is parked on it or not. Low garden benches, constructed from large pieces of Yorkstone, provide laid-back seating in which to enjoy the south-facing sunny aspect.

ABOVE Hardwearing, timeless and yet understated, Yorkstone is a garden classic. Although reclaimed stones are more expensive than new, their weathered appearance will create the impression that a path or terrace has been in a garden for decades.

LAWN

It is easy to dismiss a lawn from a small space. However, unless your garden is particularly tiny, to miss out on the smell of newly mown grass, the feel of it tickling bare feet, and, more practically, the cushioning surface for children at play, would indeed be a travesty in a family motivated space.

The lawn is at the heart of this garden. Large pieces of Yorkstone have been used as informal benches, allowing enjoyment of the south-facing aspect and providing a place to watch the children of the house at play.

PLANTING

RIGHT *Planting lavender close to a path's edge creates a wonderful welcome when you walk up to the front door, releasing its scent as you brush past. It attracts bees and butterflies too. If clipped into tight domes later in the summer its impact will continue through the winter.*

FRONT GARDEN PLANTS

A large and imposing front entrance to a property demands an equally strong planting scheme. At either side of this Yorkstone path, *Ligustrum jonandrum* lollipop topiary forms a miniature avenue, which leads the eye to the front door. The path edge is softened with lavender to create a sea of scented purple blooms at your feet. Planting either side of the path has the effect of drawing the eye away from the driveway so that attention is focussed directly on the front door.

Additional scented plants – repeated verticals of *Trachelospermum jasminoides*, with their evergreen leaves – are used around the front lawn, which balances the Yorkstone driveway opposite. Drifts of *Verbena bonariensis* and *Geranium* keep the planting scheme simple, but add a playful elegance to soften the formal look.

SCENTED CLIMBERS

Climbers are wonderful for softening structures and walls. To soften the frontage of the house and add impact to the dramatic front door, two Chinese wisteria, *Wisteria sinensis*, are planted either side of the door. Trained to run both left and right, wisteria will quickly clothe a property's walls with pendant clusters of fragrant mauve blooms in early summer, quickly followed by froths of lime green foliage, and, later in the year, long velvety green seedpods.

The wonderful scent of wisteria is accompanied by a wrap of delicious *Trachelospermum jasminoides* to the walls, which completely encloses the space. Perfect for this south-facing garden, Star Jasmine is warmed by the sun, and will release its scent into the garden. And with evergreen foliage, which turns bronzey-red in autumn, a repeat planting of *Trachelospermum* gives impact all year round.

METHOD

1 CLEARANCE AND MARK OUT

After you have cleared your garden of everything and your skip is full, use your scale plan to measure and mark out your garden components on the ground – you can do this using spray line available from builders' merchants. Walk around the ground markings, checking the width of the paths, borders and driveway for overall size, always remembering that plants will flop over onto paving taking up more space than you might have expected. Only when you are completely happy with the proportions should you finalize your material orders and start construction.

2 BOUNDARIES

It is almost always the case that you start work at the edges of your garden and work your way in. The walls in this garden are intact, but if any need replacing, now's the time to do it.

3 PAVING

Excavate the area to be paved, check your levels, then install your paths, terracing and driveway, laying all at a slight gradient so water will run off into the road, rather than back to the house. See page 163 for more information on how to lay a patio.

4 SEATING

Seating is limited to two informal Yorkstone benches. Two large slabs rest on smaller stones that form the legs of the bench. No fixing is required as the weight of the seat holds all in place.

5 PLANTING

Before preparing the planting beds, it is a good idea to fix supporting wires for the climbing plants onto the boundary walls. I always like to put horizontal wires, fixed with vine eyes screwed into the walls, all the way to the top of the wall – even if it will take a while before your climbers reach the top. This way, you won't have to clamber over and risk damaging plants when you need an extra wire mid-summer. Next, dig over your borders, adding plenty of compost or other organic matter to improve the soil. If you can afford to, ensure that all your plants arrive at the same time. Doing this allows you to plan the beds in advance, change your mind and reshuffle the order before finally planting into well prepared soil. You can add feed as you go along to the bottom of each planting hole, although I prefer to scatter fish, blood and bone over the whole area once it is planted, then immediately water it in. While this is more wasteful, it is much easier on the knees! Always finish your planting with a mulch (bark chip is perfect) to feed the soil, retain moisture, keep down weeds and give a polished professional finish. (See page 176 for details on preparing borders and containers.)

BELOW *This authentic period door, with its large round knocker, adds to the traditional feel of the space and echoes the shape of the topiary.*

MAINTENANCE

JANUARY

Repair and reshape lawn edges.

FEBRUARY

Prune wisteria, while the stems are bare, back to two buds.

MARCH

If the lawn has started to grow, mow it (on dry days only).

APRIL

Sow hardy annuals in your border gaps.

MAY

Clip your topiary, using shears or secateurs, to ensure it keeps its shape.

JUNE

Cut your grass at least once a week to ensure a thick, attractive lawn.

JULY

Shorten back wisteria shoots to five or six leaves.

AUGUST

Cut back lavender bushes. Remove flower stalks and an inch of this year's growth in the second half of August so that new shoots can grow and harden off before the first winter frosts.

SEPTEMBER

Lift and divide overgrown clumps of herbaceous perennials, replanting smaller sections to ensure all the plants in your borders keep performing well.

OCTOBER

If necessary, add more wires for climbers, training them horizontally where possible, and prune away any dead, damaged and diseased growth.

NOVEMBER

Plant tulips for a spring display.

DECEMBER

Clear up weedy beds and remove unsightly dead growth from herbaceous perennials.

ENGLISH COUNTRY GARDEN

PLANNING THE GARDEN

Set against a beautiful stone and brick house, this small, romantic country garden unifies the indoor and outdoor space, and blends in perfectly with the surrounding countryside. Unkempt, and blissfully informal, the planting enfolds a terrace that was designed to look the same age as the house; the Yorkstone paving ties in with the stone walls of the property, both in colour and texture, to create a soft, ageless and characterful garden.

DESIGN ELEMENTS

An existing wrought-iron pergola, dripping with wisteria, formed the perfect backdrop for this garden, which is inspired by the traditional country-cottage garden. The stunning views of fields beyond blend beautifully with this English country garden. A large seating area surrounded by delightfully unkempt borders, swollen with interesting perennials and heavily scented banks of lavender, creates a restful place to eat with the family, read the newspaper or simply enjoy a morning cup of coffee.

BELOW *Even in a small garden, ensure you have enough room to comfortably accommodate a table and chairs. Allow enough space to push your chair back from the table and still have room to walk through the area.*

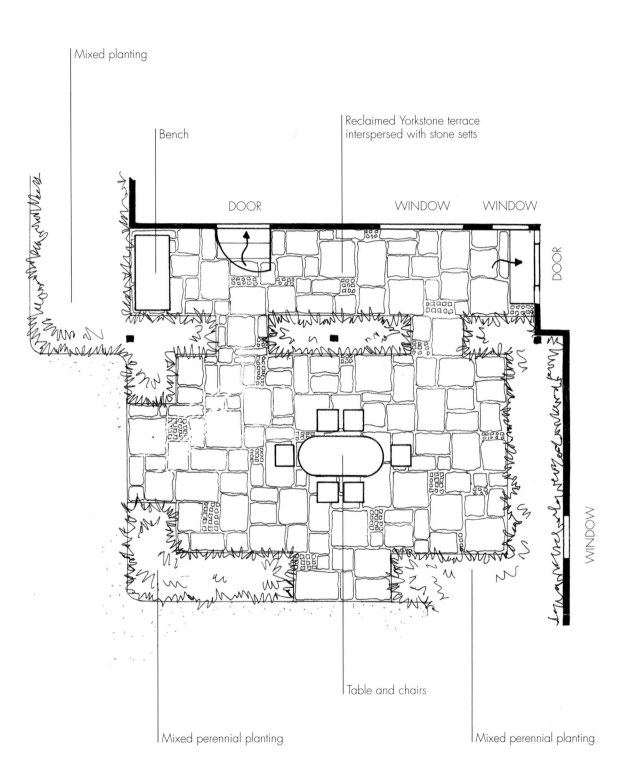

Mixed planting

Bench

Reclaimed Yorkstone terrace
interspersed with stone setts

DOOR

WINDOW WINDOW

DOOR

WINDOW

Table and chairs

Mixed perennial planting

Mixed perennial planting

WHAT YOU WILL NEED

HARD LANDSCAPING

Skip

Concrete Mixer

PAVING

MOT type 1 scalpings

Sharp sand and cement
(4:1 ratio) for mortar bed to
lay dry screed for paving

Grade 1 reclaimed Yorkstone

Marshalls Howarth Moor Sandstone
Setts in autumn bronze

Soft sand and cement mix
(4:1 ratio) for pointing paving

PLANTING

Compost

Fish, blood and bone fertilizer

Bark-chip mulch

PLANTS

Acanthus mollis

Agastache 'Summer Love'

Alcea rugosa

Alchemilla mollis

Allium 'Purple Sensation' (bulbs
studded throughout all borders)

Anemanthele lessoniana

Crocosmia 'Red King'

Digitalis ferruginea

Echinacea purpurea 'Magnus'

Gaura lindheimeri

Hemerocallis 'Stafford'

Isotoma 'Dark Blue'

Lavandula angustifolia 'Hidcote'

Liatris spicata

Monarda 'Scorpion'

Miscanthus 'Gracillimus'

Nemesia 'Confetti'

Nepeta 'Bramdean'

Nepeta sibirica 'Souvenir d'André
Chaudron'

Origanum laevigatum
'Herrenhausen'

Persicaria affinis 'Superba'

Platycodon grandiflorus

Sedum 'Gooseberry Fool'

Stipa gigantea

Stipa tenuissima

Thymus coccineus

Verbena bonariensis

Viola labradorica

*NB Measure your garden carefully, in order to establish the quantities
required to suit your particular outdoor space. Plants are usually grouped in
numbers of 3, 5 and 7, but the numbers you choose should be determined
by the size of your garden.*

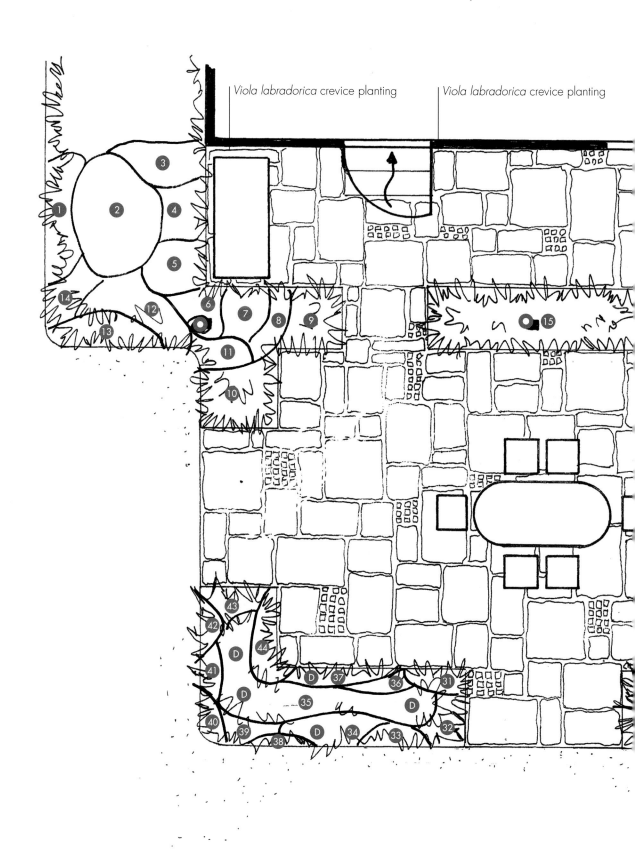

Viola labradorica crevice planting   *Viola labradorica* crevice planting

PLANTING PLAN

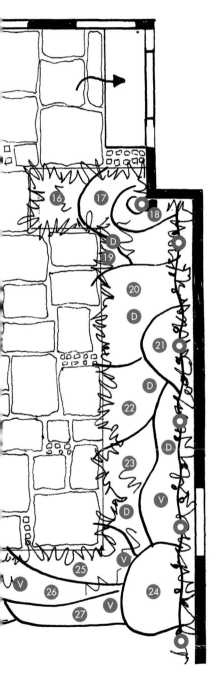

1. Anemanthele lessoniana
2. Acanthus mollis
3. Miscanthus 'Gracillimus'
4. Viola labradorica
5. Liatris spicata
6. Nepeta 'Bramdean'
7. Anemanthele lessoniana
8. Echinacea pupurea 'Magnus'
9. Lavandula angustifolia 'Hidcote'
10. Nepeta 'Bramdean'
11. Platycodon grandiflorus
12. Isotoma 'Dark Blue'
13. Persicaria affinis 'Superba'
14. Liatris spicata
15. Lavandula angustifolia 'Hidcote'
16. Lavandula angustifolia 'Hidcote'
17. Anemanthele lessoniana
18. Liatris spicata
19. Gaura lindheimeri
20. Acanthus mollis
21. Alcea rugosa
22. Sedum 'Gooseberry Fool'
23. Nepeta sibirica 'Souvenir d'André Chaudron'
24. Stipa gigantea
25. Hemerocallis 'Stafford'
26. Monarda 'Scorpion'
27. Echinacea pupurea 'Magnus'

28. Stipa tenuissima
29. Alchemilla mollis
30. Agastache 'Summer Love'
31. Agastache 'Summer Love'
32. Alchemilla mollis
33. Crocosmia 'Red King'
34. Nemesia 'Confetti'
35. Hemerocallis 'Stafford' and Monarda 'Scorpion' mix
36. Stipa tenuissima
37. Alchemilla mollis
38. Alchemilla mollis
39. Crocosmia 'Red King'
40. Stipa tenuissima
41. Alchemilla mollis
42. Origanum laevigatum 'Herrenhausen'
43. Stipa tenuissima
44. Thymus coccineus

INDIVIDUAL HIGHLIGHT PLANTS

- existing Wisteria sinensis
- Digitalis ferruginea
- Verbena bonariensis

HARD LANDSCAPING

EXISTING PERGOLA

The pergola has been integrated into the design to form a cool, covered area, providing respite from the midday sun. This has created a shady corridor, which is separated from the main paved patio by a lavender-filled bed. It also provides a wonderful viewpoint to and from the beautiful, arched entrance of the back door (which allows access into the garden). All summer the lavender provides vibrant colour and its delicious fragrance spills into the house. The blooms will prove just as irresistible to bees, too. A single teak armchair, situated close to the house, invites quiet contemplation beneath a supported canopy of wisteria, through which shafts of sunlight provide warmth and hazy views of the exuberant planting at the edges of the terrace.

OVERSIZE STEPS

The steps to the house are generously proportioned to allow easy access, but they also to provide useful impromptu seating. In a small space it's important to avoid the clutter of furniture, and it would be difficult to fit any in beneath this narrow pergola. Constructed in the same Yorkstone as the terrace, with brick risers, the steps match the detail around the doors of the property – underlining the fact that all the materials are linked.

TERRACE

Reclaimed Yorkstone has been used for centuries as a paving material. Its traditional country look is perfect for this rural setting. It is a natural sandstone with a mellow, understated tone that gives it a timeless look. One of the most successful paving designs is a random pattern using rectangular slabs of varying size. Always work from a 'key' stone and avoid straight running joints in any section of the terrace (long, straight lines will draw the eye). Perfect for large terraces, use large-scale stones to their best advantage by laying them simply and boldly. Here, to break up the expanse of terrace, and to provide detailing that attracts the eye, the occasional slab has been left out and replaced with sandstone setts. Where the house meets the terrace, a channel has been left in the paving to allow for some planting to soften the hard edges. Finally, the terrace has been laid so that any rainwater will be directed into the planting beds, an ecologically sound way to ensure the borders remain watered.

BELOW *Pergolas are a wonderful way to soften the walls of a house. Planting at the base of your pergola will extend the season of interest and soften the area where your pergola meets the ground.*

OPPOSITE *An eclectic, informal group of seats (including the outsize steps here) invites you to stop and admire the view of the garden beyond.*

PLANTING

A joyful jumble of plants in contrasting, clashing colours gives a sense of a traditional cottage garden, but with a contemporary twist. Two feature beds take centre stage within the space; a central lavender bed, set against a large bed, running along the edge of the terrace, of vibrantly clashing *Hemerocallis* 'Stafford' and *Monarda* 'Scorpion'. Other beds spill away at the boundaries in complementary tones of purple and pink.

LAVENDER BEDS

LAVANDULA ANGUSTIFOLIA 'HIDCOTE'

At the heart of the terrace, a large bank of *Lavandula angustifolia* adds a huge boost of colour during the summer months, and also encourages pollinating insects into the space to feed. Chosen for its compact nature, which ensures that foliage doesn't encroach over the paving, the dense spikes of deep violet blue over aromatic silver-grey leaves makes this the perfect lavender variety for dense hedging and borders, and path edging. Evergreen, the flower spikes should be removed in late summer, and the foliage lightly clipped into formal architectural mounds to create interest throughout the winter. In spring, clip back plants by a further 3cm (1¼in), avoiding cutting back into old wood to stop the plants from becoming too woody.

BELOW *A hidden seat wrapped with low planting creates a private space to touch, feel and breathe in the plants surrounding you.*

PERGOLA WALKWAY

VIOLA LABRADORICA

Enjoying the soft shade created by the overhead pergola, this *viola* – commonly known as Labrador Violet or Alpine Violet – is the ideal plant to soften the hard line where the paving meets the house. Pretty, heart-shaped leaves (singed with tones of plum-purple) and lilac-blue flowers are produced from May to August. An efficient self-seeder, *Viola labradorica* happily establishes itself around the garden, taking hold in paving cracks and popping up in borders in true cottage garden style.

FEATURE BED

Free-flowering plants with dramatic colour combinations are essential in the bed, which is the focus of this country garden terrace. A base mix of foliage plants, including *Stipa tenuissima* – with its fine green foliage and feathery buff flower panicles, which come in late summer – are contrasted with the felty, round leaves of *Alchemilla mollis* at ground level, and provide a backdrop to blooms throughout the season. The first plants punching through this base layer include masses of the ornamental bulb *Allium* 'Purple Sensation'. Its rich-purple balls of bloom, held aloft the foliage on stems reaching 1m (39½in) high in May and June, are replaced by the towering copper tones of *Digitalis ferruginea*, ending in a finale of colour in high summer. A jubilant drift of scarlet, lily-like blooms (*Hemerocallis* 'Stafford') intersperse with the long-flowering, vibrant, velvet purple flowers of *Monarda* 'Scorpion' to spectacular effect. Adored by bees, this purple bergamot would need support in an open border, but the under-

ABOVE *Quintessentially English,* Lavandula angustifolia *'Hidcote' has a long flowering season, but when its flowers start to go over, companion planting of late summer perennials and grasses prolong its interest.*

planting not only provides a backdrop of greenery, which intensifies the adventurous colours of the blooms above, but also acts as a prop to the stems.

SUPPORTING BEDS

Combining seed heads with the rounded shape of trimmed lavender, a handful of evergreen perennials (such as *Acanthus mollis* and *Persicaria affinis* 'Superba') and the silhouettes of grasses adds interest in the winter months. However, in this small garden, striving for year-round interest would dilute the planting scheme, resulting in a space that looks reasonable throughout the year, but lacks a period where the planting looks particularly spectacular. A mix of herbaceous perennials, with foliage that arrives early in the year, erupting into waves

of bloom (initiated by masses of the striking bulb *Allium* 'Purple Sensation'), is much more exciting. A muddle of plant heights and colliding colours creates borders alive with insects, and heady with scent. Every perennial chosen has to earn its keep, with a long season of interest, and spectacular bloom. At ground level, *Persicaria affinis* 'Superba' provides glossy evergreen foliage throughout the winter months, erupting into a carpet of low upright bloom in pink, white and red all on the same plant. Blooming from early summer through into autumn, it is perfect at the front of the border and is incredibly easy to grow. *Origanum laevigatum* 'Herrenhausen' is also in it for the long term; dusky flowers in pink and purple arrive in summer and remain intact throughout the winter, with the foliage persisting long into winter when it is mild. Mid-height pleasers include *Echinacea purpurea* 'Magnus' and *Agastache* 'Summer Love', both offering intense colour and seemingly endless bloom. If left intact, *Echinacea*'s attractive seed heads can be left through the winter to feed bird life. Add to the mix elegant, tall *Verbena bonariensis* and the border sings with colour and is alive with butterflies, right up until the first frosts of winter.

METHOD

With easy access, this small terrace is relatively easy to construct. The most difficult job is handling the reclaimed Yorkstone, which can be extremely heavy.

1 CLEARANCE AND MARK OUT

Strip out any existing lawn or terracing, and then mark the garden plan out on the ground. Transfer the various areas from your plan onto the ground using spray line (available from most builders' merchants), a scale rule and measure. Here there is no irrigation or lighting to be added, so the terrace area can be excavated to a depth that will accommodate a subbase, mortar bed and the paving (approximately 250mm/10in). Excess soil can be placed in the skip.

2 PAVING

First lay a subbase of MOT type 1 scalpings and compact with a vibrating plate compactor. Due to the varying thicknesses of the stone, every slab will have to be laid individually. Start work from a key stone laid in a corner and then spread a mix of sand and cement over the subbase. Keep varying depths to take into account the different thicknesses of the slabs. Try out the position of the sandstone setts as you go, to ensure a good fit and pattern, but do not mortar into place until the pointing stage (which takes place after the Yorkstone paving has been laid). At the terrace edges, a thick concrete haunch (a concrete bed laid on the subbase to the height of the slabs) will retain the position of the paving. This should be laid so the haunch is below the final soil level of the surrounding borders, and so is hidden from view. This negates the need for an edging strip where the terrace meets the planting beds. Finally, point the terrace with a wet mortar mix and allow to set.

RIGHT *Reclaimed Yorkstone instantly lends age and permanence to a garden terrace.*

OPPOSITE *Make borders as wide as you dare to create a terrace surrounded by an ever-changing palette of bloom.*

3 PLANTING

Once the terrace has completely set, prepare all the planting borders with a thorough dig over, removing any weeds and large stones, and then incorporating plenty of compost and food into the planting beds. All of the plants in the garden can be brought in at the same time, and laid out bed by bed. Finally, plant them into position, watering them in well and applying a generous bark-chip mulch.

MAINTENANCE

JANUARY

Start cutting back untidy grasses and herbaceous perennials that are past their best.

Order bulb catalogues for summer flowering bulbs.

FEBRUARY

Prune the wisteria, being careful not to cut off flowering buds, by reducing side shoots to two or three buds.

Divide clumps of overgrown herbaceous perennials.

MARCH

Keep an eye out for germinating weeds and remove them as soon as possible.

Lightly trim lavenders to stop them become leggy and woody.

APRIL

Annual weeds will start to pop up here and there – take them out as soon as you see them.

MAY

Feed all plants with a slow-release fertilizer.

Replenish bark-chip mulch before plants start actively growing.

JUNE

Plant up containers to add colour and interest to the terrace.

Plant summer annuals in border gaps (available from garden centres at this time).

JULY

Plant autumn flowering bulbs such as Nerine, Colchicum and Autumn Crocus.

Cut some flowers for vases indoors.

Deadhead plants to prolong their season of bloom. Hemerocallis will particularly benefit from this.

AUGUST

Prune wisteria after flowering to five or six buds from the main branch.

Keep deadheading plants, leaving grass seed heads to provide winter interest.

SEPTEMBER

Cut back faded perennials, leaving some for winter interest.

Lift and divide overgrown clumps of herbaceous perennials.

OCTOBER

Plant lily bulbs into pots on the terrace.

Plant new herbaceous perennials in border gaps.

NOVEMBER

Plant tulip bulbs to flower next year.

Continue to cut down faded perennials as you see fit.

DECEMBER

Raise containers onto feet to avoid plants sitting in winter wet.

SUNTRAP GARDEN

PLANNING THE GARDEN

To really make the best of a sunny position, why not make the garden an extension of the interior living space? Large areas of hard landscaping are the way forward, as they allow space for tables and seating, and can also incorporate sizeable planting beds. This creates interest by helping to break up the space into different zones, much like open-plan interiors. Vibrant colours and interesting textures result in an invigorating garden – an effect that is most successful in any small garden, which can cope with a blaze of flowers to enjoy at close quarters. Don't scrimp on the width of the border just because your garden is small. Make sure that beds are large enough to accommodate a range of plants that flower at varying times and give year-round interest.

To make use of every inch of outdoor space, screening an ugly view, a garage in this case, is often part of the plan. This can often be a problem in smaller gardens. A high barricade of fencing is not the best way to endear yourself to the neighbours, and with limits on boundary fence heights in most areas, installing a screen with planting of some kind is the most attractive and easy way to create privacy while blocking eyesores.

DESIGN ELEMENTS

The design layout for this garden is incredibly simple, most effective in any small space, if it is not to appear cluttered – the plants, materials and furniture provide the visual stimulus. That is not to say the scheme for the garden is without inspiration. In this rural setting, the main stimulation is the surrounding countryside, but a more contemporary edge has been added to create a rural/urban theme. This was achieved by using natural materials with 'soul' for the hard landscaping, such as the rustic slate, in colliding shades of rust red, grey and black, for the paving. The paved area is surrounded by fiery herbaceous perennials, studded with architectural evergreens, and wafting tall grasses, which form a modern meadow. An area of hardwood timber decking, tucked behind a bed, filled with veiling, tall plants, creates a little bit of privacy from which to view the whole garden.

Comfortable furniture, in proportion to the space, is worth the investment. It invites you out into the garden to relax, chat, or have dinner, and provides you with a host of different spots in which to enjoy the views – it has the effect of opening up the area and making the garden seem much larger than it really is.

LEFT *Hard landscaping is the bones of a garden, and adds year-round interest, texture and colour to a space.*

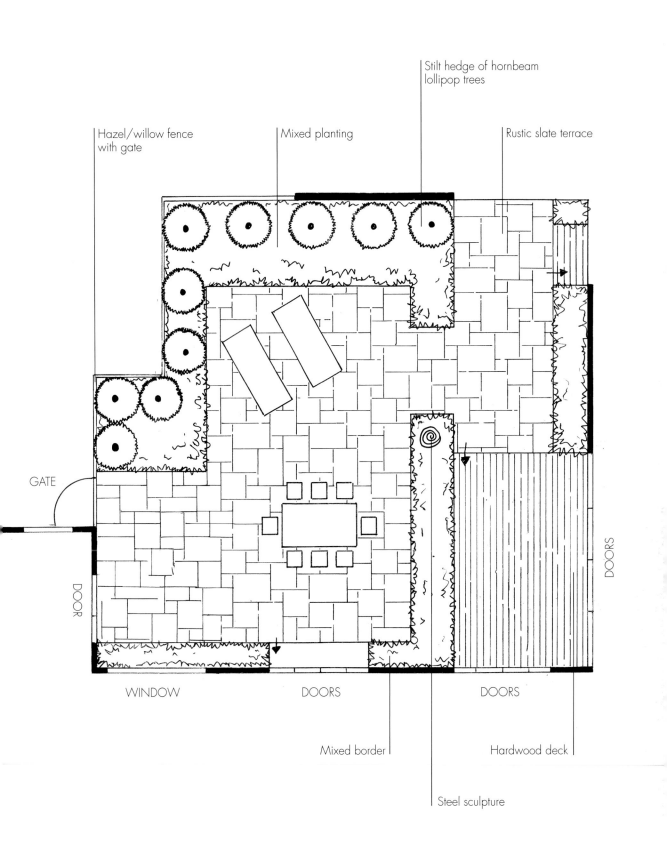

Stilt hedge of hornbeam
lollipop trees

Hazel/willow fence
with gate

Mixed planting

Rustic slate terrace

GATE

DOOR

WINDOW

DOORS

DOORS

DOORS

Mixed border

Hardwood deck

Steel sculpture

WHAT YOU WILL NEED

HARD LANDSCAPING

Skip

Concrete mixer

PAVING

MOT type 1 scalpings

Sharp sand and cement (5:1 ratio)
for mortar bed on which to
lay paving

Rustic slate

Soft sand and cement mix
(4:1 ratio) for pointing paving

BRICKWORK

Concrete footings

Mortar for brickwork

Freshfield Lane bricks

DECKING

100 x 100mm (4 x 4in) pressure-
treated timber posts for decking
frame

100 x 50mm (4 x 2in) pressure-
treated timber joists

90mm (3½in) decking frame screws

145 x 20mm (5¾ x ¾in) smooth
Balau hardwood decking boards

60mm (2⅛in) decking screws – 28
screws per square metre

Concrete to support frame posts:
ballast and ordinary Portland
cement (5:1 ratio) plus water

FENCING

Hazel wands and stakes (woven *in
situ* by a specialist)

IRRIGATION

Micro irrigation with computerized
timer. Available in kit form
from garden centres and
Internet suppliers.

Irrigation timer

Low-pressure porous pipe

Tap connectors

Solenoid valves

Pipe pegs

LIGHTING

Hunza adjustable spotlights in
powder-coated finish

Hunza wall downlights in powder-
coated finish

Low voltage, black, powder-coated
spike lights

Cables, clips and other accessories.

Transformers

Junction boxes

Remote control

*NB You will need to measure your garden carefully in order to establish the
quantities required to suit your particular garden. All lighting to be installed by
a qualified electrician.*

PLANTING

Achillea 'Inca Gold'

Agapanthus campanulatus var. *albidus*

Agapanthus Headbourne Hybrids

Ajuga reptans

Alchemilla mollis

Astelia chathamica

Bergenia cordifolia 'Winterglut'

Carpinus betulus, 20–25cm (8–10in) trunk circumference hornbeam lollipop standards with 1.8m (5¾ft) clear stem minimum

Crocosmia 'George Davidson'

Crocosmia 'Red King'

Euphorbia mellifera

Echinacea purpurea 'Magnus'

Geum 'Fire Opal'

Hedychium coccineum 'Tara'

Hedychium gardnerianum

Helenium 'Rubinzwerg'

Hemerocallis 'Stafford'

Heuchera cylindrica 'Greenfinch'

Kniphofia 'Nancy's Red'

Lysimachia ciliata 'Firecracker'

Miscanthus sinensis 'Malepartus'

Oxalis 'Sunset Velvet'

Persicaria amplexicaulis 'Atrosanguinea'

Phormium 'Platt's Black'

Potentilla 'Gibson's Scarlet'

Rudbeckia fulgida 'Goldsturm'

Trachelospermum jasminoides tripod

Veronicastrum virginicum 'Temptation'

AROUND THE DECK

Achillea millefolium 'Red Velvet'

Astelia chathamica

Digitalis ferruginea

Geum 'Fire Opal'

Hemerocallis 'Stafford'

Potentilla 'Gibson's Scarlet'

Stipa tenuissima

Verbena bonariensis

NB Plants are usually grouped in numbers of 3, 5 and 7, but the numbers you choose should be determined by the size of your garden.

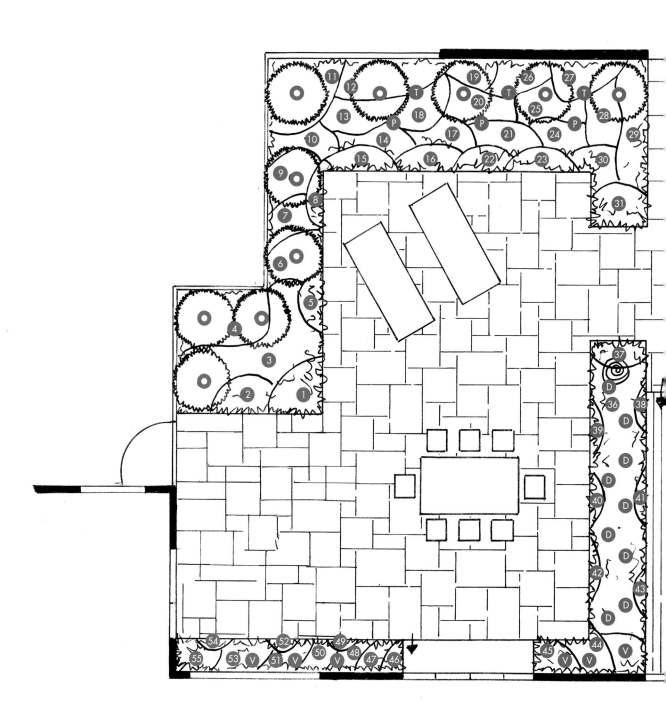

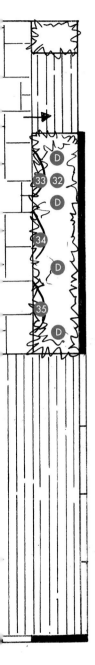

PLANTING PLAN

1. *Astelia chathamica*
2. *Hemerocallis* 'Stafford'
3. *Lysimachia ciliata* 'Firecracker'
4. *Miscanthus sinensis* 'Malepartus'
5. *Hemerocallis* 'Stafford'
6. *Rudbeckia fulgida* 'Goldsturm'
7. *Echinacea purpurea* 'Magnus'
8. *Ajuga reptans*
9. *Achillea* 'Inca Gold'
10. *Hemerocallis* 'Stafford'
11. *Euphorbia mellifera*
12. *Miscanthus sinensis* 'Malepartus'
13. *Crocosmia* 'George Davidson'
14. *Helenium* 'Rubinzwerg'
15. *Alchemilla mollis*
16. *Geum* 'Fire Opal'
17. *Crocosmia* 'Red King'
18. *Persicaria amplexicaulis* 'Atrosanguinea'
19. *Hedychium gardnerianum*
20. *Kniphofia* 'Nancy's Red'
21. *Agapanthus campanulatus albidus*
22. *Heuchera cylindrica* 'Greenfinch'

23. *Potentilla* 'Gibson's Scarlet'
24. *Agapanthus* Headbourne Hybrids
25. *Veronicastrum virginicum* 'Temptation'
26. *Persicaria amplexicaulis* 'Atrosanguinea'
27. *Persicaria amplexicaulis* 'Atrosanguinea'
28. *Hedychium coccineum* 'Tara'
29. *Lysimachia ciliata* 'Firecracker'
30. *Bergenia cordifolia* 'Winterglut'
31. *Astelia chathamica*
32. *Hemerocallis* 'Stafford'
33. *Potentilla* 'Gibson's Scarlet'
34. *Geum* 'Fire Opal'
35. *Potentilla* 'Gibson's Scarlet'
36. *Hemerocallis* 'Stafford'
37. *Astelia chathamica*
38. *Potentilla* 'Gibson's Scarlet'
39. *Geum* 'Fire Opal'
40. *Potentilla* 'Gibson's Scarlet'
41. *Stipa tenuissima*
42. *Stipa tenuissima*

43. *Geum* 'Fire Opal'
44. *Achillea millefolium* 'Red Velvet'
45. *Stipa tenuissima*
46. *Stipa tenuissima*
47. *Achillea millefolium* 'Red Velvet'
48. *Helenium* 'Rubinzwerg'
49. *Oxalis* 'Sunset Velvet'
50. *Lysimachia ciliata* 'Firecracker'
51. *Hemerocallis* 'Stafford'
52. *Oxalis* 'Sunset Velvet'
53. *Potentilla* 'Gibson's Scarlet'
54. *Oxalis* 'Sunset Velvet'
55. *Helenium* 'Rubinzwerg'

INDIVIDUAL HIGHLIGHT PLANTS

D = *Digitalis ferruginea*

V = *Verbena bonariensis*

P = *Phormium* 'Platt's Black'

T = *Trachelospermum jasminoides* tripod

O = *Carpinus betulus* hornbeam lollipops

HARD LANDSCAPING

ABOVE *Plants spilling from surrounding borders soften the hard landscaping. The natural colours of the plants and blooms are echoed by the varying tones of the paving, which bind this garden together as a cohesive whole.*

PAVING

Your choice of paving will often inform the style of your garden. In a small garden, a paved terrace will undoubtedly take up much of the surface area, allowing maximum use with a minimum of upkeep. Here, wide borders form the periphery of the garden, with an additional planting bed cutting through the paving at one side. This screens off a slightly more private deck, which is hidden behind tall planting and accessed from inside via large sliding doors.

Although slate is finely grained and very uniform in texture, it is craggy at the edges and is available in varying tones – not just the familiar grey so often used in interiors. Here a playful colour base of grey, shifting into ochre and red, creates a multi-tonal, warm, rustic floor that gives the garden depth. It also reflects seasonal shifts, particularly the autumnal tones of the surrounding woodlands, creating interest throughout the autumn and winter, long after the impressive garden furniture has been stored away.

A random laying pattern in varying slab sizes contributes to the feeling of informality, with a light pointing grout between each slab to give a crisp, professional feel.

DECKING

With various doors and sliding windows leading from different rooms of the house out into the garden, there is an opportunity to provide distinct seating areas to suit particular moods. The timber deck, which is separated from the main paving by tall herbaceous perennials, allows for a change in mood and style. Hardwood boards, laid with a step up from the surrounding paving level, create further interest and separation; as the decking is laid horizontally, across the line of vision, it slows down the pace, helping to create an area in which to relax.

WOVEN HAZEL BOUNDARY

When is a fence not just a fence? When it is an expertly woven hazel structure built by local craftsmen using traditional techniques. An attractive sculptural gate and boundary fence is much more desirable than simply

BELOW *The upright stems of the hornbeam lollipop standards dramatically rise up from informal planting to add definition to the scheme, and a great contrast to the horizontal weave of the surrounding hazel fence.*

plumping for the ubiquitous larch-lap variety. Here, a continuous weave of coppiced hazel rods and chestnut poles enhances the rural/urban look of the garden. Weaving on site will allow for the strongest fence, as well as forming a beautiful line that is flexible enough to accommodate changes in direction through the curve of the weave. Hazel is woven around chestnut upright posts that have been cemented 60cm (23½in) into the ground for maximum strength. Once erected, hazel fencing becomes an instant windbreak, less likely to blow down than sawn-lap panels, and the attractive rustic appearance is particularly effective in less formal settings. Panels can be used rather than the continuous weave method, but although they are available in various heights, they are usually only available in 1.8m (6ft) lengths. Moreover, the required fence posts between panels can be very obvious and corners can be difficult to accommodate.

Hazel hurdles also have environmental benefits as they are made from coppiced wood; choosing them, as opposed to chemically treated softwood panels, continues to sustain an ecologically valuable habitat, provides rural employment, adds to the local *genus loci* and calls for fewer conifer plantations.

BRICK RETAINING WALLS

Whether holding back a challenging hillside or making sense of an uneven back yard, it is unusual to find a completely flat garden, and it is amazing how often a sloping or bumpy garden needs a retaining wall. The secret is to make sure that the wall blends into, and becomes part of, the garden; essential constructional work should not dominate the space. If you are using bricks, as here, the obvious and best way to do this is to match them exactly to those of the house. It is then a good idea to add a planting border in front of the wall to soften the hard lines that will inevitably be created.

LIGHTING

To best enjoy alfresco soirees, ambient lighting is a must. Lights pick out areas that are not noticed in daylight; hard landscaping features can become sculptural in their own right and distinct moods can be created through different effects. Textures and tones of brickwork can be highlighted through an effect called 'grazing' (uplighting so light spreads over a vertical surface), and favourite structures and plants can be 'up lit' or 'down lit' for emphasis. In this garden, the topiary 'lollipop' hornbeams are an obvious choice to light up. A number of circuits (independent strings of light fittings, each with

ABOVE *A coping stone in the same slate as the terrace, laid atop the retaining wall, protects the brickwork and forms a shelf for candles and other accessories.*

their own power supply) are needed, so that different lights can be flicked on and off at whim. The thrill of using outdoor lighting is in the ability to change the ambience of your space. Windows become frames through which to view a whole new world, which is beautiful not just in summer but also throughout the seasons. When dusk falls, lighting can transform your garden into an area where everything is fresh, dramatic and intriguing.

IRRIGATION

Outside taps are essential in any garden. However, if the responsibility of remembering to water your garden fills you with fear, an irrigation system is a sensible investment. A 'leaky pipe' system (a thin pipe perforated with tiny holes running through the borders fixed to a timer on any outside tap) is sufficient for most gardens. They are easily hidden from view in a flowerbed, with a sensible covering of mulch, and can move from one border to another. If you are planning to do this, conduit piping should be installed beneath any hard landscaping at the construction stage. As with lighting, by installing solenoid valves and extra timers, you can turn on or close off the water in different zones at will.

PLANTING

SOFT LANDSCAPING

Energizing, frolicsome and exuberant planting, with a nod to the wild, was the plan for the herbaceous perennials in these borders. Bold colours and year-round interest from flowers, foliage and seed heads, both evergreen and deciduous, keep the garden looking attractive and, at the same time, soften large areas of hard landscaping. This has been achieved through the use of deep borders that provide enough space for a wide range of plants. Although this kind of planting is not for the low-maintenance gardener, who could fail to be charmed into caring for such a bounteous display? A line of lollipop-trained topiary hornbeams overlooks the garden, which lends maturity and anchors the quirky planting scheme.

HORNBEAMS

Mature topiary hornbeams are used at the garden boundaries for several reasons. Large specimens planted side-by-side form a stately and attractive living screen, blocking out unattractive views beyond (in this case, a large garage). Almost sculptural, topiary pieces are classically elegant, lending the garden weight and an upper storey by lifting the eye along the stem to make the garden seem bigger than it really is. When lit up after dark (by uplights), they become breathtakingly architectural, taking centre stage away from the planting that is dominant in daylight hours. They also attract wildlife; great care was taken in checking for nests before giving the trees their first clip in spring.

HOT GARDEN COLOURS

In the small garden, where space is limited, planting can afford to pack a punch. There is no better way to create interest and a sense of excitement in a border than by using hot colours, which may overpower other planting in a larger space. Energizing, effusive and exciting, reds, oranges and yellows collide to create an attractive, bright and enthusiastic scheme. In mid summer, easy-to-grow *Hemerocallis* 'Stafford' produces new flowers continuously, and, although each bloom only lasts a day,

they arrive in such quick succession you would be forgiven for not noticing. To get the most from this vibrant scarlet daylily, plant it in bold drifts and deadhead it regularly to ensure an even longer blooming season. *Lysimachia ciliata* 'Firecracker', with its nodding, sunny yellow blooms, adds to the scene. While the flowers are bold, the dusky purple foliage adds depth and variety; the shadowy colour of the foliage echoes the sword-shaped leaves of the evergreen *Phormium* 'Platt's Black'. With its bright red flowers, *Potentilla* 'Gibson's Scarlet' dances at the front of the border, beneath blue *Agapanthus*

BELOW *A stainless-steel sculpture reflects the colours of the garden, bounces light into the small space and adds year-round up-thrust to the scheme.*

and the long, slender tapers of *Persicaria amplexicaulis* 'Atrosanguinea' at the rear of the scheme. Later in the season, *Rudbeckia fulgida* 'Goldsturm', *Helenium* 'Rubinzwerg' and *Echinacea purpurea* 'Magnus' will ensure that the heat in the border is kept turned up.

EVERGREEN PLANTS

Hot schemes work best when they have a backdrop of foliage to perform against. Green leaves frame bold blooms and intensify the heat of the flower, and, although they play a supporting role in the border, they are beautiful in their own right. Here, one of the main contributors is *Miscanthus sinensis* 'Malepartus', a tall, handsome upright grass, with mid-green foliage that changes to the red, russet and gold tones of autumn just

ABOVE LEFT *A swathe of green foliage in the background adds informality to the scheme, whilst keeping weeds down and intensifying the colour of blooms in flower.*

ABOVE RIGHT *Rustic slate adds an earthy naturalness to this garden, while its warm rusty tones reflect the landscape beyond the confines of the space.*

as its silky flowers of reddy brown begin to fade away. *Euphorbia mellifera* is a more robust supporter, valued here for its evergreen leaves reaching up to 2m (6½ft) in height. Although grown primarily for its foliage, its lime green flower bracts have a honey scent, which is enhanced by the confined nature of the small garden. Finally, attractive *Astelia chatamica*, with its silvery spear-shaped foliage, is planted at the ends of the borders as a visual full stop to the meadowy vibrancy of the blooms.

METHOD

1 CLEARANCE AND MARK OUT

As always, the first thing required in creating your new garden is to clear out anything you don't want to keep. This can be hard work if, for instance, you have an existing terrace to remove. If this is the case, it's a good idea to remove the paving slabs first and to investigate the foundations to see if they are good enough to reuse. Often they can be, and a few test excavation holes will reveal whether your subbase is worth keeping, even if it needs topping up. Once you've cleared the site, mark out with spray line (available from builders' merchants) the new garden areas, checking that they are all large or small enough to suit your needs.

2 RETAINING WALL

Here, a retaining wall is required to support the garden where it slopes towards the house. The foundations and the wall are formed from bricks that match exactly those of the house. If you need a retaining wall, it should be built at this stage.

3 LAYING CONDUIT PIPES

Before carrying out any hard landscaping (paving), lay conduit piping to protect electrical cables and irrigation hoses, positioning it so that it reaches the borders and the various parts of the garden. If these are not laid first, then areas of paving may have to be lifted. It is advisable to use a professional when setting up an outdoor electrical system.

4 PAVING

Excavate and make level the area to be paved. Arrange for the foundation materials to be delivered. Lay the slate on a mortar bed (see page 163) and leave it to 'go off' (set) before pointing the joints. In this garden, large steps leading up to the French windows have been added to give easy access to and from the garden. Generous steps were also chosen because they could double up as an impromptu seating area.

ABOVE *Planting stretched in front of a secondary decked seating area divides up the space. A steel sculpture, echoing the form of the* Astelia chathamica, *provides a visual full stop at the end of the planting border.*

5 DECK

Once the paving is laid, construct the decking (see page 164). In this garden, the level of the deck is slightly higher than the main paved area. This creates interest and, along with the planting bed down its longest side, helps to separate the different seating zones.

6 PLANTING MATURE TREES

Before the hazel boundary fencing can be installed, the large mature hornbeam trees should be planted. These will be very, very heavy, requiring at least four people to lift them into position. When buying mature trees, their size, height, spread and weight should be a consideration. You may need easy side or back access to the garden. If access is only through the house (as is often the case in small urban gardens), you probably won't be able to get these trees into the space without a crane, let alone plant them! Once the trees are in their planting holes, check that all the stems are in line and vertical, using a spirit level, if necessary, before backfilling.

ABOVE *Woven hazel fencing is perfect for rural spaces, forming a link between the cultivated garden within its confines and the rural space beyond.*

BELOW *Planting mature trees gives instant impact to a space. These lollipop hornbeams tolerate wet, clay soils and hold their leaves well into the winter making them perfect for screening.*

7 FENCING AND GATE

Once all the major works have been completed, and an open access to the site is no longer required, the fencing and gate can be erected. Here, local craftsmen constructed the hazel fence in continuous weave. (See page 166 if you are constructing a panel fence.)

8 BORDER PREPARATION

With the trees and the fencing in position, prepare the borders by thoroughly digging them over, adding plenty of compost and feed ready for planting (see page 176).

9 PLANTING

Lay out the remaining plants and then plant them in their final positions.

10 FINAL ELECTRICS, IRRIGATION PIPES, MULCH

Make sure that the lighting is wired in and irrigation pipes are laid before applying a mulch over all the borders. This will act as a weed suppressant, and food and water retainer for the plants, while also masking any unsightly irrigation pipes.

MAINTENANCE

JANUARY

Keep the crowns (above-ground growth) of perennials free of leaves falling from the mature hornbeams – it will stop them rotting.

FEBRUARY

Order bright summer flowering bulbs to add to the herbaceous borders – lilies will add scent, Tigridia will add colour and Nerines will add interest to the beds later in the season. Plant them as soon as they arrive in early spring.

MARCH

Lift and divide any clumps of herbaceous perennials that begin to get too big for your borders. New plants can be used to fill gaps or be given away to friends.

APRIL

Add stakes to support taller growing perennials – much easier to do now before they begin growing.

Turn on your irrigation system.

MAY

The hornbeams will need to be given the first of their twice-yearly cuts to keep them in shape.

JUNE

Plant containers of summer bedding, herbs and tumbling tomatoes, to add further interest to the terrace areas.

JULY

Deadhead blooms in the herbaceous border to keep plants flowering for as long as possible.

AUGUST

The topiary hornbeams will need a second cut before the trees produce buds for the new leaves in the following year. If you have left it too late and you can clearly see the buds, either trim very lightly, avoiding the removal of as many buds as possible, or leave the trimming until next year.

SEPTEMBER

Cut back to ground level any unsightly dead growth from herbaceous perennials. Start planting spring-flowering bulbs, such as crocus and daffodils, to give early interest next year.

OCTOBER

When other plants have gone into hibernation, plant a winter-flowering climber, such as Clematis cirrhosa, among new ivies to give interest to the retaining wall at the rear of the main border.

NOVEMBER

Protect plants from frost with a thick layer of protective mulch.

DECEMBER

Make any repairs required to the hazel boundary fencing while the flowering plants are dormant.

Turn off your irrigation system.

LOW-MAINTENANCE GARDEN

PLANNING THE GARDEN

The owners of this tiny garden, squeezed between rows of terraced houses in the heart of the city, were keen to regain some outdoor space; somewhere to enjoy with friends and a place relax after a long day at work. Low-maintenance gardens tend to be those that can be left to tick over gently by themselves, without much input from their owners. Truly successful ones need to pack a punch in the summer and stay looking good right through the winter, which can be a difficult balance to achieve in a small space.

The first thing to consider in the low-maintenance garden is the inclusion of a lawn. Lawns rarely look convincing when squeezed into small spaces. They often seem compressed, are impractical for tables and chairs, and the high volume of traffic they have to withstand can rapidly turn their soft green lushness into threadbare shabbiness. Add a shower or two and it can quickly become a mud bath. Doing away with the lawn completely is a vastly time-saving solution. It eradicates the once-weekly cut (and often twice weekly during the growing season), frequent edging, autumn maintenance of spiking, scarifying, seeding and feeding – not to mention the headache of where to store the lawn mower and other gardening tools required. It is usually much wiser to invest in a smart area of paving that requires nothing more than the occasional sweep and hose down.

Plants used should be unfussy and mass planted, and pretty much able to look after themselves. Shrubs, particularly evergreens, are low-maintenance garden stalwarts, offering year-round interest through foliage, bark and the occasional bloom. An irrigation system can further spare the not too green-fingered, or indeed forgetful, gardener the guilt of a desiccated, dead border or pot plant, while outdoor lighting extends the garden's interest into the night.

ABOVE *Even in the tiniest of spaces, zoning a garden into separate areas can create the illusion that a garden is much bigger than it is. Here a simple step separates two very different seating areas.*

DESIGN ELEMENTS

This contemporary and elegant low-maintenance space has been planned on a limited budget. As is so often the case in towns, privacy is a huge issue. Large extended properties, many with first floor balconies, can overlook and overpower small gardens. Here, the clients wanted to dispense with this claustrophobic feeling and to create as large a feeling of space as possible. An uncluttered, minimalist design appealed, with built-in, multi-functional furniture to circumvent storage issues in winter. To tackle the issue of privacy, a wrap of elegant black bamboo was used. The tall bamboo created a garden ready for extensive entertaining, while avoiding the possibility of agitated glances from next-door neighbours.

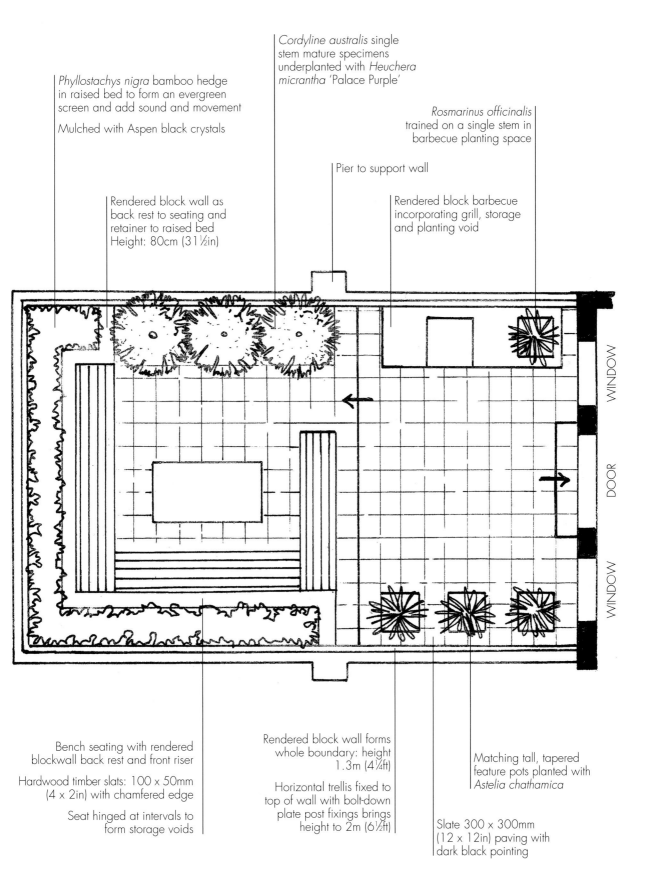

Cordyline australis single stem mature specimens underplanted with *Heuchera micrantha* 'Palace Purple'

Phyllostachys nigra bamboo hedge in raised bed to form an evergreen screen and add sound and movement

Mulched with Aspen black crystals

Rosmarinus officinalis trained on a single stem in barbecue planting space

Pier to support wall

Rendered block wall as back rest to seating and retainer to raised bed Height: 80cm (31½in)

Rendered block barbecue incorporating grill, storage and planting void

WINDOW

DOOR

WINDOW

Bench seating with rendered blockwall back rest and front riser

Hardwood timber slats: 100 x 50mm (4 x 2in) with chamfered edge

Seat hinged at intervals to form storage voids

Rendered block wall forms whole boundary: height 1.3m (4¼ft)

Horizontal trellis fixed to top of wall with bolt-down plate post fixings brings height to 2m (6½ft)

Matching tall, tapered feature pots planted with *Astelia chathamica*

Slate 300 x 300mm (12 x 12in) paving with dark black pointing

WHAT YOU WILL NEED

HARD LANDSCAPING

PAVING

MOT Type 1 scalpings to 100mm (4in) depth

Full mortar bed of sharp sand and cement at 5:1 ratio

Marshalls' midnight-blue slate paving

Pointing – mix soft sand and cement at 4:1 ratio

BENCHES

90 x 28mm (3½ x 1⅛in) Meranti hardwood slats

100 x 50mm (4 x 2in) treated tanalised softwood frame

100 x 100mm (4 x 4in) Meranti hardwood legs

BARBECUE

Concrete blocks

Soft sand and cement mortar

Concrete render

1 x concrete lintel

Marshalls' midnight-blue slate paving

Paint

Metalwork – bespoke stainless-steel grills

Stainless-steel angle irons

LIGHTING

Low-voltage, black, powder-coated spike lights

Cables, clips and other accessories

Transformers

Junction boxes

Remote control

IRRIGATION

Irrigation timer

Low-pressure porous pipe

Tap connectors

Solenoid valves

Pipe pegs

NB Measure your garden carefully, in order to establish the quantities required to suit your particular outdoor space. All lighting to be installed by a qualified electrician.

PLANTING

Feature pots for *Astelia*

Compost

Slow-release fertilizer

Stone-chipping mulch

PLANTS

Astelia chathamica

Cordyline australis single-stem mature specimens

Heuchera micrantha 'Palace Purple'

Phyllostachys nigra

Rosmarinus officinalis trained on a single-stem (for barbeque planting space)

NB Plants are usually grouped in numbers of 3, 5 and 7, but the numbers you choose should be determined by the size of your garden.

HARD LANDSCAPING

Even the tiniest of low-maintenance gardens can be interesting and stimulating spaces. A simple design with crisp, clean lines will give the garden clarity. This layout is supported by carefully considered components that unify the garden. Using a limited plant palette that takes up a small amount of surface area also cuts down on the upkeep. Zoning the garden for different uses adds interest, and a simple step splits the garden into two distinct areas; the entertaining zone with repeat planting as a backdrop to seating, and the culinary zone with a large built-in barbecue. Creating a change of level in any garden will make the space more interesting and, in a small garden, can make it appear infinitely larger.

FENCING

As the largest vertical element separating you from your neighbours, or the street, fences can easily dominate small gardens. In towns and cities, different parties often own them and, consequently, they can be made of different materials on each side. Nothing brings down a garden like a shabby old fence. If you've got a decrepit fence along one side, and you're unsure as to whether it is your responsibility, check your deeds and speak to your neighbours. If it is their liability, try to convince them that it makes sense to replace it with something fresher, more secure and more contemporary than the ubiquitous, larch-lap panel. However, if you can arrange for all your fencing to be replaced in the same material, so much the better – you'll end up with a uniform boundary, as opposed to a mismatched hotch potch.

Here, simple board fencing is used – the vertical lines at the garden's periphery lead the eye upwards to the sky when glimpsed through the bamboo planted in front.

zones. This flow of material creates the illusion of space,
ABOVE *Simple benching with a minimum of support allows paving to reach uninterrupted to the planting beds, so visually extending the terrace.*

PAVING

Due to the tiny proportions of this garden, most of the area was paved in midnight-blue slate. Slate lends depth and richness to a garden, and its dense texture and crisply cut edges keep it looking fresh and modern. Because all of the garden can be seen from the house, the whole area has been paved in the same material. To avoid monotony, interest has been added by including a step up to a slightly higher level, which creates two

which could have been lost if contrasting materials had been chosen for each area.

Although traditionally used in cottage gardens, the dark solid look of slate has become increasingly popular as a contemporary paving, especially since the advent of standard-sized slabs. The large size of these slabs makes a bold statement and contradicts the common belief that small, modular paving works better in small spaces. Making sure that every component works, both proportionally and practically, is crucial to the success of any small garden. This garden meant planting beds close to the fence on three sides of the paving, so accurate measuring was essential. In any garden, but particularly small ones, it is important that patios are large enough to accommodate a table and chairs comfortably, allowing a chair to be pushed back away from the table and for a person to pass behind it. A space of 3 x 4m (10 x 13ft) should be sufficient.

Gravel has been used as planting mulch; it is a similar colour to the slate so this also visually extends the ground area through the planting to the boundary line.

BENCHES

Where individual chairs and a table would clutter up a small garden, built-in seating becomes an architectural and sculptural feature; giving the garden focus while maximizing space. Constructed in hardwood, to give them longevity, these benches can be left outside permanently, even in winter. Made on site, the long, low proportions of the benches give the garden a contemporary feel. Their bespoke dimensions provide the maximum possible seating within this small plot, ensuring that not an inch of garden space is wasted. The cost of having them built is comparable to buying a patio set for six. In order to exploit the limited space, the benches are constructed with a minimum of supports, so that they appear to float above the paving, which runs beneath the benches' plane and makes the ground area appear as large as possible.

BARBECUE

If you want to entertain and host lots of parties in your garden, it will need a focus. A barbecue, which can double up as a heat source, is ideal for this purpose. The barbecue in this garden is constructed from concrete blocks, which are rendered and painted. It has surfaces at either side to accommodate trays of food and cooking utensils. Three apertures for stacked wood not only provide fuel ready to burn on the barbecue's fire shelf, but also look attractive. The sides and preparation surfaces are made of slate, which is practical and ties in well with the paving, while the barbecue's front face is painted with a vibrant colour to add a startling contrast to the rest of the garden's muted palette. As for the cooking area itself, three sliding shelves of various sizes allow food to cook at different rates, or keep food warm when cooked. At one end – added for fun – there is a

small area for plants. Here, a specimen single-stem trained rosemary is perfect – you can collect stems for kebabs or add to the coals to release an appetizing aroma. If you're considering building a barbecue, always err on the large size, especially as regards the cooking surface – coals can be concentrated at one end of the firebox, if necessary, but you can't make a small barbecue any bigger. It is worth investing in stainless-steel shelves that will not rust if they are left outside permanently, and the overall height of the barbecue should be at least 1m (3ft), if you are to cook and prepare food with ease. Keeping the barbecue close to the house makes it easy to carry food and equipment in and out of the kitchen. Finally, always ensure that surrounding structures, which could potentially become fire hazards, are protected.

LIGHTING

Lighting adds a new dimension to a garden, particularly for those who often don't arrive home until after dark. Here, lighting is capable of transforming the garden and giving it an alternative mood and appearance. The space can be enjoyed well into the evening in summer, and appreciated from inside during winter. In a small garden, a low-voltage system is perfectly adequate, as the light will be concentrated within the space. Always ensure that a qualified electrician installs your lighting.

IRRIGATION

An irrigation system is essential if you are the type of gardener who could easily forget to water your plants, or if you work long hours and don't want the responsibility, or hassle of getting the hose out after a tiring day. Bamboo is both hungry and thirsty so, as the main component of the planting, it is essential that it be protected. An irrigation system is an insurance policy for your plants' health, a time saver, and is useful if you are often away from home. The important thing to remember is that if your irrigation hose needs to cross areas of hard landscaping before it reaches your borders, then a section of conduit pipe should be laid at construction stage to allow your system to run unseen below your paving. If not, installing a system is simple: fit a timer to your tap, connect a hose (with an end-closure fitting to stop the flow of water) to the tap and lay the hose around the garden. Finally, a layer of mulch on planting beds to disguise the pipe will give a professional finish without compromising the system.

PLANTING

It makes sense to use vertical space in a small garden; tall, narrow plants take up a minimum of floor space and will add height to the garden. Because the eye is drawn upwards to the sky, the whole space will appear larger as a result. A limited plant palette of architectural evergreens will make your plants easy to maintain and look good all year round.

CORDYLINE AUSTRALIS
(SPECIMEN PLANT BORDER)

With tall, elegant stems and massed heads of arching sword-like leaves, the three specimen plants create maximum impact. Planted side by side in this small space, they erupt skyward to great architectural effect. This is investment planting, and although the initial cost may seem high – as plants this size have been cared for and brought on by a nursery for a number of years – the ratio between age of plant and cost is low. The *Cordylines'* evergreen foliage not only acts as a focal point, but also gives a degree of privacy from the mass of properties overlooking the space from all sides. A huge froth of unusual scented bloom appears in summer, to add to the wonderful foliage effect. Little maintenance is required, except a regular feed in spring and autumn with slow-release fertilizer, and removing dead leaves from the base of the crown as the plant grows. It should also be mentioned that although this plant is not considered completely hardy when young, a mature specimen can tolerate several degrees of frost, which in the city, as here, is rarely a consideration.

BAMBOO
(BAMBOO SCREENING)

Phyllostachys nigra makes a wonderful screen, creating dense privacy in this urban garden. New green shoots age quickly to burnished black, and the canes thicken up quickly. Bamboo is evergreen, but each spring it drops a number of leaves to replenish its foliage. This should not in itself be a concern, but be aware that with bamboo planted en masse as here, there can be considerable sweeping up of spent foliage. Every two or three years, thin and remove smaller, weaker canes, and strip away foliage from the base of the plants to reveal the outlines and colour of the canes to full effect. If the height becomes overwhelming, you can prune your bamboo into a more traditional hedge shape. However, once trimmed, a bamboo cane will not put on new growth from the tip, and although new canes will grow taller than the existing hedge height, judicious cutting is required. It is best to remove the canes that have grown too high at ground level and prune the tips of only a few very high canes to maintain a natural look.

ASTELIA CHATHAMICA
(TALL PLANTERS)

Echoing the foliage of the statement cabbage palms (*Cordyline australis*) opposite, the handsome clumps of silver-leaved *Astelia chathamica* are raised up to eye level in three matching statement pots to provide balance and drama in this shadier spot of the garden. There are very few architectural plants that will grow happily in the shade and are also tolerant of dry conditions; this plant grows naturally upon cliffs and rocky ground, so will naturally tolerate the restricted root development that you would expect from containers.

RIGHT *Benches provide seating for large groups, double up as tables for nibbles and allow horizontal lounging to read the papers on a sunny Sunday morning!*

METHOD

A tiny space can make garden landscaping more complicated than usual, so good planning and organization are key. Too many people can result in chaos as folk trip over each other to complete the work. Progress will also be slower if the only access to the garden is through the house.

1 CLEARANCE AND MARK OUT

If you only have access through the house, before any of the clearance begins, it is important to protect floors and any difficult-to-negotiate corners in the house. Retain as much of the existing hard landscaping material as possible. Recycling it as a hard-core base for the new paving not only saves labour (and backs!) in carrying materials out of the garden, but also the cost of skips, and of buying new foundation materials. In addition, if kept on site, this waste product will not contribute to landfill sites. Here, much of the material was crushed and compacted into the subbase foundations for the new paved areas – including the slightly raised area accessed by a step. Mark out the garden using spray line (available from most builders' merchants). Next, scale rule and measure, to transfer the garden areas from the plan onto the ground.

2 BOUNDARIES

It is important to replace boundary fencing as soon as possible, in order to provide a boundary line for the hard landscaping to run up to. Fencing is the first priority in any garden project, and if yours needs replacing or repairing, do it at the earliest opportunity.

3 LIGHTING AND IRRIGATION

If you choose to install lighting, it's always best to call upon a qualified electrician to carry out the 'first fix'; if you are employing a landscape contractor to build your garden, they will almost certainly organize this for you. Electric cables, conduit pipes and irrigation hardware will need to be put in position before your paving is laid.

4 PAVING

Slate paving is laid in the same way as any other stone (see page 163), but, because slate tiles are very thin compared to most slabs, it is advisable to lay them on a full mortar bed to ensure that all slabs are fully supported. Carefully point between the slabs once they have set solid.

5 BENCHES

Construct the feature timber benches (here, they were done by on-site carpenters) before the beds are prepared and planted. This allows access all around the bench area during construction.

6 BARBECUE

Working from a plan, build the barbecue on top of the new slate paving in the lower terrace. Work will take place over a few days to allow the mortar joints that hold the concrete blocks together to set, before rendering and painting. Fix the surface slate on the food preparation areas and fit the stainless-steel box and trays.

7 PLANTING, IRRIGATION AND FINAL ELECTRIC FIX

Prepare all of the beds by digging over and then incorporating plenty of compost and plant food into the ground. Move the pots into position, fill with a drainage layer of gravel and then fill with compost to just below the lip. Large plants will need to be planted before the lighting and irrigation pipes can be installed. Lastly, add a thick layer of stone-chipping mulch.

OPPOSITE *A built-in barbecue is a fun focal point in this garden, painted an eye-catching cerise-plum colour to echo the colour of the* Heuchera *planted alongside.*

MAINTENANCE

Even the most low-maintenance spaces require *some* looking after. Although it is not necessary to carry out all of these jobs every year, this section provides a guide on what to look out for.

JANUARY

Ensure that all irrigation lines are drained to prevent freezing water from damaging them.

FEBRUARY

Service your lighting system, replacing wiring, bulbs or lamps, if necessary.

MARCH

Sweep up spent foliage dropped from the bamboo, as evergreen leaves are replenished.

APRIL

Turn on your irrigation system when plants begin actively growing.

MAY

When new growth appears and all danger of hard frosts has passed, cut back frost-damaged branches on the Cordyline australis specimens to just above the newly formed shoots.

Feed all plants with a slow-release fertilizer.

JUNE

Plant up containers of summer bedding to ring the changes and add seasonal colour and interest.

JULY

Replenish stone chippings around the plants, if necessary.

AUGUST

Midway through the season, it is a good idea to pressure wash your paving to remove ingrained dirt and algae and keep it looking good.

SEPTEMBER

Apply a wood preservative to the fence, if necessary, while the weather is still dry.

OCTOBER

Clean and store away additional garden furniture if you don't intend to use it through the winter.

NOVEMBER

Clean your barbecue if you don't intend to use it until spring. Repaint it if necessary.

DECEMBER

Turn off your irrigation system while plants are dormant. Remove the timer, too, to protect it against winter weather.

RUSTIC FAMILY GARDEN

PLANNING THE GARDEN

Inspired by rural spaces, most especially meadows, this garden was planned to be in harmony with nature. It is a welcoming, informal, laid-back space where plants rule the roost. An almost overwhelming, kaleidoscopic collision of bloom, foliage and colour provides a sensory feast, supported by hard landscaping built purely from timber as a frame to the borders. Sustainability is also a key theme. Materials are sourced as locally as possible to ensure the minimum of environmental impact. Plants are chosen to be appropriate for their position, to require a minimum amount of water and be self-feeding (composted garden and kitchen waste can be used in the garden), while wildlife is actively encouraged. This family space includes a large lawn, some homegrown vegetables and a trampoline to entertain the children – and possibly the adults, too!

DESIGN ELEMENTS

This garden is split into two halves: an upper terrace leading directly from the house and a lawn area in the lower garden, which is reached by steps. This east-facing garden loses the sun from the main terrace area by early afternoon, but catches the sun in the far left-hand corner at the back of the garden towards the end of the day. A large terrace next to the house is perfect for breakfasting and evening soirees, and an informal area of benching at the end of the garden is ideal for enjoying the last rays of sunlight. The benches also provide a wonderful view when looking back through the vegetable patch and wider garden towards the house. Splitting the garden into separate zones provides interest and different spaces in which to sit and reflect. Separating each area with exuberant high plantings ensures that the garden isn't viewed all at once, providing intrigue and inviting one to explore. Zoning also allows different groups of people to use the garden at the same time, but within separate spaces. These individual areas give a degree of privacy, which is especially effective in a small garden.

RIGHT *A generous area of decking to the rear of the house creates a low-maintenance outdoor room suitable for parties of adults or children, and lots of family fun.*

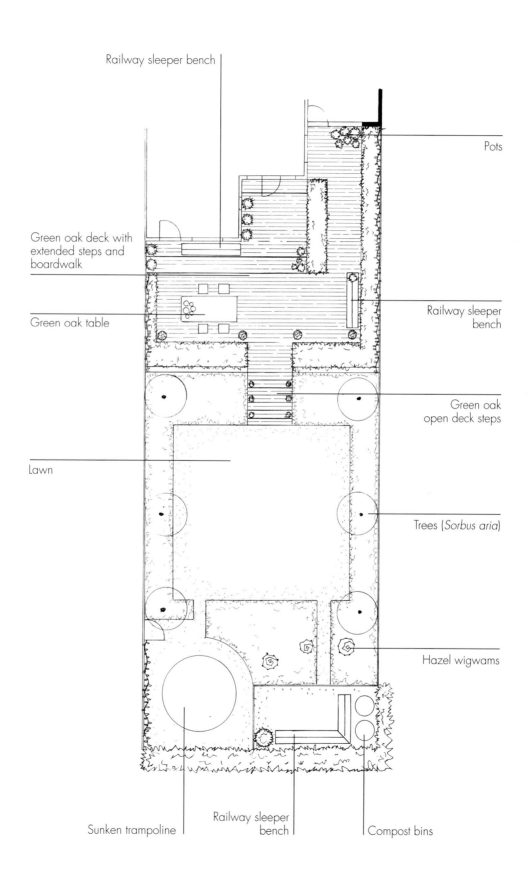

Railway sleeper bench

Pots

Green oak deck with extended steps and boardwalk

Green oak table

Railway sleeper bench

Green oak open deck steps

Lawn

Trees (*Sorbus aria*)

Hazel wigwams

Sunken trampoline

Railway sleeper bench

Compost bins

WHAT YOU WILL NEED

HARD LANDSCAPING

RETAINING WALL

Concrete for foundations

Treated tantalized softwood railway sleepers

300mm (12in) Timberlok screws

Geotextile filter membrane, fixed with nails

Right-angled steel straps, to support corners

Treated timber batons

Stainless-steel woodscrews

DECKING

100 x 100mm (4 x 4in) posts concreted into the ground

Postfix ready-mix concrete to concrete vertical support posts. 1 x 20kg bag will fill a hole 30 x 30 x 30cm (12 x 12 x 12in). Use 40kg of concrete per post.

100 x 50mm (4 x 2in) joists for decking

150 x 20mm (6 x ¾in) sawn green oak decking boards

100mm (4in) galvanized nails to secure all frameworks. Use a framing nail gun to speed up the installation.

60mm (2⅓in) trim-head screws to fix decking to joist framework – 28 screws per metre

Exterior grade marine ply to support planting beds within the deck area

DECK STEPS

3.5m x 75mm x 350mm (11ft x 3in x 13¾in) stringers

150 x 20mm (6 x ¾in) sawn green oak decking boards

60mm (2⅓in) finishing trim-head screw to fix decking to stringers and batons

50 x 25mm (2 x 1in) oak batons

BARK CHIP AREA

Fence posts to act as an edge for bark-chip mulch

Timber pegs to hold fencepost into position

Screws to fix posts

Weed-proof landscape membrane

Bark-chip mulch

Railway sleepers

300mm (12in) Timberlok screws

BENCHES

Railway sleepers

300mm (12in) Timberlok screws

TABLE

150 x 20mm (6 x ¾in) rough-sawn green oak decking boards

60mm (2⅓in) finishing trim-head screws

Single piece of air-dried green oak

NB Measure your garden carefully, in order to establish the quantities required to suit your particular outdoor space.

PLANTING

Compost

Fish, blood and bone fertilizer

TOP DECK

Achillea 'Feuerland'

Agastache 'Summer Love'

Anemanthele lessoniana

Angelica gigas

Crocosmia 'Jackanapes'

Deschampsia cespitosa 'Golden Dew'

Dierama pulcherrimum

Echinacea purpurea 'Magnus'

Geranium 'Patricia'

Helenium 'Moerheim Beauty'

Hemerocallis 'Stafford'

Liatris spicata

Monarda 'Scorpion'

Nepeta 'Walker's Low'

Origanum laevigatum 'Herrenhausen'

Pennisetum alopecuroides 'Hameln'

Salvia nemorosa

Sanguisorba obtusa

Sedum 'Herbstfreude'

Stachys monieri 'Hummelo'

Stipa gigantea

Trifolium rubens

Verbena bonariensis

IN POTS

A variety of herbs

Mixed sempervivum

Buxus sempervirens balls

Coreopsis verticillata 'Grandiflora'

Cosmos atrosanguineus

Miscanthus sinensis 'Ferner Osten'

Phyllostachys nigra

Strawberry varieties

LOWER GARDEN

Anemanthele lessoniana

Anthriscus sylvestris 'Ravenswing'

Broad beans

Calamagrostis brachytricha

Coreopsis verticillata 'Grandiflora'

Courgettes

Cut-and-come-again salad mix

Digitalis 'Alba'

Dwarf French beans

Echinacea purpurea 'Magnus'

Foeniculum vulgare

Hemerocallis 'Stafford'

Knautia macedonica

Lavandula angustifolia

Lychnis chalcedonica

Miscanthus 'Gracillimus'

Monarda 'Cambridge Scarlet'

Nepeta 'Walker's Low'

Potato 'Anya'

Santolina chamaecyparissus

Sisyrinchium striatum

Sorbus aria

Stipa gigantea

Sunflowers: 'Giant Single' and 'Velvet Queen' seeds

Sweet peas: 'Cupani' seeds

Tomato 'Hundreds and Thousands'

Verbena bonariensis

Veronicastrum virginicum 'Fascination'

Veronicastrum virginicum 'Temptation'

CLIMBERS

Akebia quinata

Clematis 'The President'

Cobaea scandens

Lonicera periclymenum 'Graham Thomas' and 'Belgica'

Trachelospermum jasminoides

NB Plants are usually grouped in numbers of 3, 5 and 7, but the numbers you choose should be determined by the size of your garden.

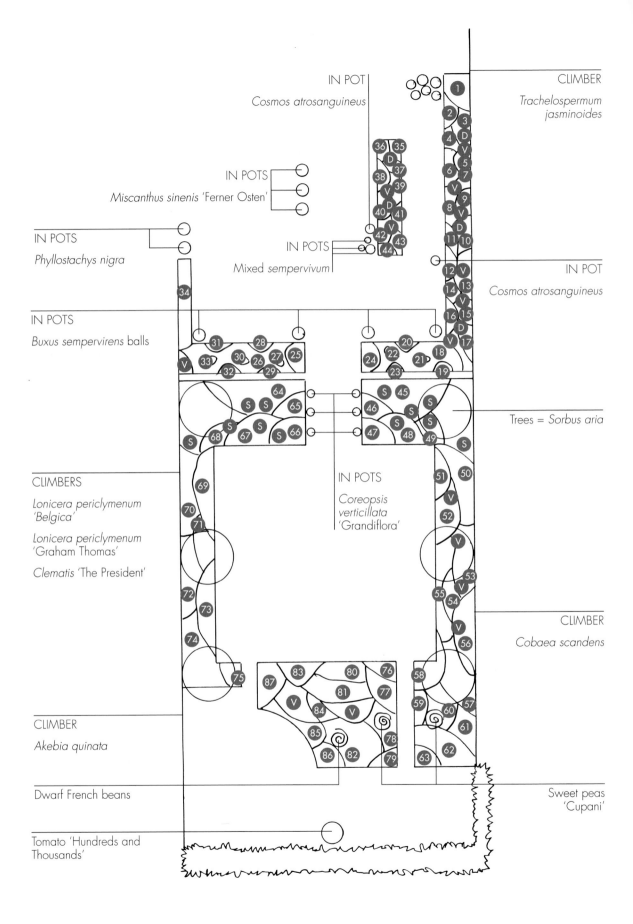

IN POT

Cosmos atrosanguineus

CLIMBER

*Trachelospermum
jasminoides*

IN POTS

Miscanthus sinenis 'Ferner Osten'

IN POTS

Phyllostachys nigra

IN POTS

Mixed *sempervivum*

IN POT

Cosmos atrosanguineus

IN POTS

Buxus sempervirens balls

Trees = *Sorbus aria*

CLIMBERS

*Lonicera periclymenum
'Belgica'*

*Lonicera periclymenum
'Graham Thomas'*

Clematis 'The President'

IN POTS

*Coreopsis
verticillata
'Grandiflora'*

CLIMBER

Cobaea scandens

CLIMBER

Akebia quinata

Dwarf French beans

Sweet peas
'Cupani'

Tomato 'Hundreds and
Thousands'

PLANTING PLAN

1. *Angelica gigas*
2. *Trifolium rubens–*
3. *Deschampsia cespitosa* 'Golden Dew'
4. *Geranium* 'Patricia'
5. *Sanguisorba obtusa*
6. *Salvia nemorosa*
7. *Stipa gigantea*
8. *Stachys monieri* 'Hummelo'
9. *Achillea* 'Feuerland'
10. *Nepeta* 'Walker's Low'
11. *Sedum* 'Herbstfreude'
12. *Geranium* 'Patricia'
13. *Stipa gigantea*
14. *Agastache* 'Summer Love'
15. *Achillea* 'Feuerland'
16. *Origanum laevigatum* 'Herrenhausen'
17. *Monarda* 'Scorpion'
18. *Anemanthele lessoniana*
19. *Echinacea purpurea* 'Magnus'
20. *Echinacea purpurea* 'Magnus'
21. *Liatris spicata*
22. *Liatris spicata*
23. *Echinacea purpurea* 'Magnus'
24. *Pennisetum alopecuroides* 'Hameln'
25. *Pennisetum alopecuroides* 'Hameln'
26. *Anemanthele lessoniana*
27. *Liatris spicata*
28. *Echinacea purpurea* 'Magnus'
29. *Echinacea purpurea* 'Magnus'
30. *Liatris spicata*
31. *Echinacea purpurea* 'Magnus'
32. *Echinacea purpurea* 'Magnus'

33. *Liatris spicata*
34. *Crocosmia* 'Jackanapes'
35. *Geranium* 'Patricia'
36. *Deschampsia cespitosa* 'Golden Dew'
37. *Hemerocallis* 'Stafford'
38. *Sedum* 'Herbstfreude'
39. *Helenium* 'Moerheim Beauty'
40. *Hemerocallis* 'Stafford'
41. *Sedum* 'Herbstfreude'
42. *Helenium* 'Moerheim Beauty'
43. *Stipa gigantea*
44. *Origanum laevigatum* 'Herrenhausen'
45. *Miscanthus* 'Gracillimus'
46. *Monarda* 'Cambridge Scarlet'
47. *Coreopsis verticillata* 'Grandiflora'
48. *Lychnis chalcedonica*
49. *Sisyrinchium striatum*
50. *Veronicastrum virginicum* 'Temptation'
51. *Calamagrostis brachytricha*
52. *Hemerocallis* 'Stafford'
53. *Foeniculum vulgare*
54. *Stipa gigantea*
55. *Santolina chamaecyparissus*
56. *Veronicastrum virginicum* 'Fascination'
57. *Hemerocallis* 'Stafford'
58. *Nepeta* 'Walker's Low'
59. *Lavandula angustifolia*
60. Cut-and-come-again salad mix
61. Potato 'Anya'
62. Broad beans
63. *Lavandula angustifolia*

64. *Miscanthus* 'Gracillimus'
65. *Monarda* 'Cambridge Scarlet'
66. *Coreopsis verticillata* 'Grandiflora'
67. *Lychnis chalcedonica*
68. *Calamagrostis brachytricha*
69. *Anemanthele lessoniana*
70. *Digitalis* 'Alba' and *Anthriscus sylvestris* 'Ravenswing'
71. *Hemerocallis* 'Stafford'
72. *Echinacea purpurea* 'Magnus'
73. *Anemanthele lessoniana*
74. *Digitalis* 'Alba' and *Anthriscus sylvestris* 'Ravenswing'
75. *Lavandula angustifolia*
76. *Nepeta* 'Walker's Low'
77. *Echinacea purpurea* 'Magnus'
78. Cut-and-come-again salad mix
79. *Lavandula angustifolia*
80. *Knautia macedonica*
81. *Stipa gigantea*
82. Courgette
83. *Echinacea purpurea* 'Magnus'
84. *Echinacea purpurea* 'Magnus'
85. Mixed herbs
86. *Lavandula angustifolia*
87. *Lavandula angustifolia*

INDIVIDUAL HIGHLIGHT PLANTS

S = Sunflowers: 'Giant Single' and 'Velvet Queen'
V = *Verbena bonariensis*
D = *Dierama pulcherrimum*

HARD LANDSCAPING

RETAINING WALLS

If you live on a sloping site and you're considering a deck, a retaining wall be your first priority. Here, railway sleepers were chosen to replace the existing wall, as a good-looking, cost-effective option. Solid, long lasting and full of character, a railway sleeper wall is simple to construct. Retaining walls need to cope with an excessive amount of weight and pressure, so vertical sleepers will add further support to horizontally stacked sleepers, as well as adding interest. Generous, wide planting beds can be prepared at lawn level as well as at the edge of the higher deck. This will help to camouflage the retaining wall and provide a buffer zone to keep people away from the edge. Given time, the sleeper wall itself will weather to an attractive silver-grey colour.

GREEN OAK DECK

With plenty of knots and an elegant grain, oak lends an air of permanence and character to a deck, which is not always found in the uniform grain of the popular, tropical, hardwood decks. British oak is not fast-grown, and will last for hundreds of years, even outliving the time the oak has taken to grow. Oak gets harder with age and has been used in construction for centuries, so by using oak you are creating a link with the past, making it a particularly apt choice for this rustic garden.

BELOW A meadow planting style is the perfect foil to green oak decking. The two work hand in hand to create a rustic, natural look.

Green oak is unseasoned, and is said to be green for up to five years after it has been felled. It holds a high moisture content, and, as it slowly dries out, the oak will gently crack and move as it gets harder and stronger, with most shrinkage occurring across the width of the board rather than the length. Although these splits and 'shakes' add to the character of a deck, the natural shrinkage of the boards demands careful attention when laying and fixing. Unusually, green-oak decking boards are butt jointed (laid side by side without an expansion gap) when fixed to the supporting joist frame beneath, and gaps will naturally form as the boards contract. Also be aware that the tannins in oak may corrode some types of metal screws, and also react with some fixings to produce a dark blue stain through the timber, which is impossible to remove. To this end, it is wise to always use stainless-steel screws, preferably with a small head size, which will retract into the wood's surface and eventually be lost to view. Green-oak decking is mostly available as a sawn product and is beautifully suited to rustic gardens, where some variation in board size and shrinkage are acceptable. Rough-sawn boards show all the natural character of English oak, but they are more cost effective than seasoned planed boards and give a degree of slip resistance. Wonderful to work with and exquisite to behold, British oak is known for its depth of colour and tone, which in time ages to a weathered silver-grey.

TRAMPOLINE

Although trampolines have become increasingly popular in recent years, due to their overall bulk and invariably bright blue colour, siting a trampoline in a small garden can be extremely difficult. Plumping for a dark green surround to the central black mat is a more pleasing choice. Digging out a trench, into which the legs of the trampoline will be embedded, makes the trampoline easy for children to use, negates the need for a safety net and allow it to blend discretely into the garden. Situated behind a bank of veiling planting further dilutes the visual impact, while adding a degree of privacy; something as important to children as it is to adults.

BELOW Trampolines have become ubiquitous garden accessories for families, and yet they can be very ugly. Green surrounds blend better, while sinking them into the ground makes for low visibility, easy access and safe play.

PLANTING

GRASSES

A wonderful addition to the small garden, grasses create a sense of rhythm and movement in borders, billowing and flowing when caught in the slightest breeze to give a feeling of openness and space. Linked intrinsically with natural planting style, they offer structure to meadow-inspired plantings. Their long season of interest – combined with their shape, form, texture and subtlety of colour – provides a wonderful backdrop to more dramatic plantings of herbaceous perennials, which come and go throughout the growing season. Clump-forming evergreen *Anemanthele lessoniana* is used in a wide bed at the top of the retaining wall. This provides a bank of movement in shades of olive green, which transform, as the lax flower panicles are produced, into rusty shades of reddy orange. Undemanding and low maintenance, the grasses provide a wonderful edge to the oak deck. *Echinacea purpurea* 'Magnus' and *Liatris spicata* punch through the grassy veil to provide seasonal interest and pinpoints of colour, livening up the summer scene and providing a link to surrounding herbaceous perennials.

HERBACEOUS PERENNIALS

If you are looking for a natural planting scheme, choose herbaceous perennial plants for the individual beauty of their blooms. They provide a long season of interest, and are able to attract beneficial insects, such as bees, wasps and butterflies. Additionally, a willfully wild, densely planted scheme will minimize maintenance and create an ever-changing, colourful border.

A herbaceous perennial is a non-woody plant that dies down completely in the winter; the roots remain alive below ground ready to thrust up new growth in the spring. This means that there is constant change and replenishment in the garden, which is important in a small space. Create borders as wide as you dare so that they can accommodate groups of plants in front of one another, giving depth of interest and variety of bloom.

A swathe of *Trachelospermum jasminoides* climbing the boundary fencing provides an evergreen, scented backdrop for the golden, shimmering flowerheads of giant oat grass (*Stipa gigantea*), which can reach over

ABOVE *Layers of planting create a whimsical, laid-back scheme. Here wiry stems hold aloft tight buds of* Cosmos atrosanguineus, *which unfold into seemingly impossibly large blooms of dusky red that release the delicious scent of vanilla and chocolate when warmed in the sun. The perfect family garden plant.*

2m (6½ft) in height in one season. In turn, this swaying grass provides the tall growing perennials with an enhancing and lightly wafting veil. Height is provided in the borders with sumptuous, velvety purple bracts of the bee balm *Monarda* 'Scorpion' and statuesque, beetroot-red domes of *Angelica gigas*, which elegantly smoulder while adding structure. Endlessly flowering, *Verbena bonariensis*, bounces throughout the garden, and all these lofty perennials attract a host of bees and butterflies, along with plenty of colour. All the plants look wonderful when backlit in shafting sunlight. Mid-level plantings include *Helenium* 'Moerheim Beauty', with its richly toned, copper-red (daisy-like) flowers, threading through with the soft, hair-like foliage of the grass, *Stipa tenuissima*.

ANNUALS

Annuals are an ideal way of creating an established look in a very young garden, because their life cycle is completed in one year. They must germinate, grow, flower and seed at a rate of knots so are perfect for adding bulk while more permanent plantings are becoming established. Just as with herbaceous perennials, greater impact will be created by using banks of plantings, but where I recommend using perennials in groups of five or seven in the small garden, annuals can be used in higher numbers.

At the base of the retaining wall, sunflowers are the perfect choice to camouflage the sleepers, giving them a chance to weather and age, and the other plantings time to get going. A mix of two varieties creates a sunflower sea of bloom, The typical, sunny yellow *Helianthus annuus* 'Giant Single' can grow several metres within a season, making it the perfect project for the children in the household to grow. The only problem with these large sunflowers is that the tumultuous growth results in just one single flower head. Although each bloom is spectacular, combining this with *Helianthus annuus* 'Velvet Queen' will extend the sunflower forest's interest, adding gorgeous, multiple flower heads up the stem in rich, velvety shades of crimson, ochre and orange. Both are spectacularly easy to grow: simply sow seed, spaced roughly 45cm (18in) apart, into a well-prepared border in April and keep them well watered. They make excellent cut flowers, if gathered just before the heads are fully open, but, if left on the plant, birds enjoy the seed heads that follow the bloom.

BELOW *Growing sweet peas with children is fun. Easy to grow and quick to flower, children will particularly enjoy constructing the teepees that encourage their growth.*

ABOVE *The intense colour tones of Monarda 'Scorpion' rise above aromatic foliage to give height, scent and drama in mid to late summer.*

VEGETABLES

There's room for a few fruit and vegetables in any garden, no matter how small. Do what cottage gardeners have been doing for centuries and mix them in with your flowering plants. Grow lettuce as an edging along the front of borders, or create a temporary 'hedge' of beans by growing French and runner beans up a home-made trellis – in this garden we used hazel sticks in a wigwam form tied with raffia. This will provide pretty flowers and tasty produce. Close to the house, we planted strawberries in hanging baskets, while the oak table is well stocked with a containerized herb garden – a pretty accompaniment to alfresco dining.

METHOD

If you want to make your garden sustainable, be sure to reuse as many materials as possible from your previous garden. You could build the sleeper retaining wall in front of an existing retaining wall, then fill the void between the two with all the generated compacted rubble. And the deck could be laid onto existing paving, with upright frame support posts punching through the existing hardcore into the ground, held firmly in place with concrete.

1 CLEARANCE AND MARK OUT

Try to keep clearance relatively simple, as much of the construction can be built around or on top of existing structures. Marking out is next, using spray line (available from most builders' merchants). Scale rule and measure, to transfer the plan onto the ground.

2 RAILWAY SLEEPER RETAINING WALL

Dig holes to house the six upright sleepers that will help take the pressure put upon the retaining wall from the soil behind it. It is important that these are entirely vertically, and also that they are completely in line with each other, before finally setting them into the ground with concrete. (Sleepers can be extremely heavy, so make sure you have an extra set of hands before attempting to move them.) Stack the railway sleepers in layers butting up to the upright verticals, working from the front corners in. Each sleeper needs to overlap the cut edges of the sleeper below. They also need to be fixed securely with long screws that are countersunk, ensuring that the they penetrate the underlying sleeper to a reasonable depth – a minimum of 50mm (2in). Typically, these fixings are

positioned 150mm (6in) in from each end of a timber, with six equally spaced screws holding the sleepers in position in a zigzag down the length of each sleeper. Once the wall is finished, nail a geotextile membrane on the inside to stop soil seeping from behind.

3 DECKING AND BOARDWALK

In this garden a large frame was constructed above the existing terrace, supported by vertical posts concreted at key points into the ground. Before the oak boards are laid, fix marine ply boards at the front edge of the frame. This will accommodate planting beds at the edge of the deck and soften the hard landscaping. Lay the boards, butt jointed and held in position with a clamp, before screwing them to the frame. (See page 164 for more information on decking.)

4 OPEN DECK STEPS

Move the left and right stringer (the sloping board that supports the ends of the steps) into position to rest upon the top of the retaining wall. A 'bird's mouth cut' (90°) at the top of each stringer will ensure a nice tight fit where they meet the wall. Hold them in place with timber fixings. At ground level, sink the stringers into a hole at least 900mm (35½in) in length. Ensure that the hole is packed with gravel around the timber base to aid drainage. (NB All cut ends should be treated with wood

LEFT *Symmetrical planting at the top of the steps leading to the lower garden is augmented by pots of clipped* Buxus sempervirens, *which also frame the view beyond.*

RIGHT *Open steps leading down onto the lawn create the perfect space for a child's den below. Alternatively, fill the space with ferns and other shade lovers.*

preservative.) Backfill the hole with layers of soil, compacting each layer as you go. Next, calculate the number of steps and the height of the rise, marking the measurements out on both left and right stringers, taking into account the thickness of the tread. Move a central stringer into position and fix. Make sure that the other stringers are parallel. Transfer the measurements of the step treads and risers from the side stringers to the middle one, using a level or a tape measure, then cut out the position of the treads and risers. This will give you the shape of the staircase. The amount cut away from the central stringer may seem excessive, but, once the treads are fixed into position and are level, the structural rigidity will be regained. Fix batons to both side stringers on the markings for the treads; these will support the decking boards to form your steps. Finally, fix deck boards to these batons and over the central cut stringer for a sturdy, attractive staircase.

5 TRAMPOLINE

To sink your trampoline into the ground, first ensure that the ground where you are installing it is completely level. Next, dig out trenches for the legs. Though not essential, it is wise to lay thin concrete foundations to support the weight of the trampoline. Remember that the final ground level needs to be approximately 50mm (2in) less than the height of the trampoline. This allows for a gap to release the air that is dispelled when children are jumping. After the legs are installed, backfill the trenches with soil. While the bounce mat is off, dig a large central hole the same depth as the height (above ground) of the trampoline. Make sure that the hole has sloping sides so that they don't collapse, and then cover the hole with a weed-proof membrane. Fit the bounce mat and get jumping! The quickest way to dig the trenches and holes is by using a mini-digger, but you can dig by hand. Use the excess soil to level the central lawn area.

6 LAWN

To level the area, spread excess topsoil from excavating the trampoline pit over the existing lawn. Tread it down by walking over the area, placing one foot in front of the other. The first time you do this, you'll probably find some humps and dips, which can be removed by giving the surface a light raking. Repeat the treading down. When the area is completely level give it a final rake, then sow grass seed over the area at a rate of approximately 35g per square metre. Lightly rake in and keep well watered.

ABOVE *A small area of lawn allows for football, tennis and general play. Until the children leave home, stripes will exist only in your imagination!*

7 BARK CHIP AREA

Once the lawn level is established, turn your attention to the area at the bottom of the garden. A bark chip area is easily constructed by applying a weed-proof membrane over the space, running just beneath fenceposts laid horizontally at ground level and screwed into position to timber pegs hammered into the ground. Fix the membrane behind the posts with U-shaped nails. Then simply scatter bark chip to a depth of 50mm (2in) over the entire area.

8 PLANTING

Dig over all of the beds and borders, add compost and feed, including large quantities of compost-blended topsoil to the built-in beds around the decking. Attach climbing support wires to the fencing before planting the climbers into position. Taking them off the canes and tying them onto the new support wires will ensure good, even growth. Next, lay out and arrange all the plants prior to planting. Cover all of the planting beds with a mulch, which will not only act as a weed suppressant, soil conditioner and water retainer, but also give a good, professional finish.

9 TABLE

A professional carpenter was commissioned to make the rustic oak table, but if you want to make something similar, this is the general method. Oak was used in order to match all the other timber detailing within the garden. Source your tabletop before beginning construction, as this will dictate its design. Large, single sections of timber such as this can be found at most sawmills, who will be happy to sort through their stock to find the perfect piece for you. The trestles were made with leftover pieces of decking board. They were constructed as a simple A-frame, with a shelf held in position by stainless-steel fixings. To keep the tabletop from cupping, fix a large section of timber batoning 75 x 75mm (3 x 3in) across the centre width. The table can be sanded or left rough-sawn, according to your requirements.

BELOW *Ensure your table is large enough to accommodate your family and friends, and perhaps even a tabletop container herb garden.*

10 RAILWAY SLEEPER BENCHES

These are simple to construct and comprise two railway sleepers placed side by side on two short legs. The legs are cut 100mm (4in) narrower than the width of the seat (these were constructed from off-cuts from the retaining wall). Simply place the sleepers on top of the legs and screw each one home with 300mm (12in) Timberlok screws. The same technique was used to form an L-shaped bench at the bottom of the garden.

BELOW *Leftover railway sleepers are easily recycled to form chunky garden benches. Airy planting behind them softens their impact.*

MAINTENANCE

JANUARY

Plant summer flowering bulbs such as Galtonia, Gladioli and Triteleia.

Hang bird feeders to attract birds into your garden.

Plant bare root shrubs to add cost-effective structure to the lower garden.

Water the bamboo in containers, if the weather is particularly dry or windy.

Chit seed potatoes.

FEBRUARY

Cut back the grasses in your garden, including Anemanthele lessoniana.

Plant lilies in pots, so that they will add scent and colour in summer.

Get a head start on flowering by sowing sweet peas in pots on your windowsill.

Plant fruit trees and bushes in the bottom section of the garden.

MARCH

Cut back herbaceous perennials.

Add supports to plants such as Veronicastrum and Sanguisorba before they begin growing.

Plant out any new herbaceous perennials that have taken your fancy.

Sow hardy annuals, such as sunflowers, Rudbeckia and annual poppies.

Give the lawn a first cut, setting the blades high.

Plant out early potatoes.

Sow lettuce, peas, spinach, beetroot and plant onion sets directly into the ground.

APRIL

Thin out hardy annual seedlings sown last month.

Layer climbers by bending stems to touch the ground, and pinning them into place with wire. Water well, and by next year you will have new plants to bulk up your fence line with bloom.

Begin regularly removing weeds from your borders.

MAY

Water plants in dry weather.

Plant hanging baskets as summer bedding becomes available in garden centres, but avoid planting until all chance of frost has passed.

Thin out your bamboo, removing the older canes rather than young.

Plant dahlias to add to the riot of colour and for cut flowers for the house too. Dahlia 'Rip City', D. 'Hillcrest Royal' and D. 'Magenta Star' all pack a punch.

Direct sow runner beans, climbing beans, sweetcorn, courgette and marrows.

Give plants a feed with a slow-release fertilizer, such as fish, blood and bone.

Top up mulch in your borders.

JUNE

Watch out for aphids on soft new growth.

Regularly mow the lawn, neatening up the edges with shears.

Keep up with the weeding.

Plant tomatoes out in the garden.

JULY

Deadhead flower borders to keep all plants blooming for as long as possible.

Regularly harvest vegetables and keep them well watered.

AUGUST

Enjoy your garden by eating out in it as much as you can!

Deadhead summer bedding plants and hanging baskets.

Keep new areas of lawn well watered during dry weather.

Keep harvesting vegetable crops.

SEPTEMBER

Begin planting autumn flowering bulbs such as Alliums, Chionodoxa and Scilla.

Cut back herbaceous perennials that are past their best.

OCTOBER

Rake up fallen leaves from the lawn.

Re-seed bare patches of lawn and carry out autumn lawn maintenance – such as scarifying, aerating and feeding.

Plant onion and garlic sets.

NOVEMBER

Plant tulip bulbs at this time.

Plant gaps in borders with new herbaceous perennials.

Bring in pots of herbs to the greenhouse, or indoor windowsill, to prevent them freezing in winter weather.

DECEMBER

Trim deciduous hedging at the bottom of the garden.

Order seed for next year.

NIGHT GARDEN

PLANNING THE GARDEN

Like so many town houses that are split into separate dwellings, this garden is situated to the rear of a large house. The owner lives on the first and second floors of the property, so it is therefore extremely important that the garden looks as interesting from above as it does from ground level. Size is an issue here, so by breaking the space up into different zones, accessed by boardwalk paths, the garden becomes more interesting and seems infinitely larger than it really is. The garden is overlooked and receives very little sun, so privacy and light are paramount considerations here. However, low light levels provide the perfect opportunity to give a garden a tropical feel, offering the owner an soothing refuge from the city. Using large specimen palms, instant impact can be created, combined with upward lift among informal drifts of smaller plants, which will swell and grow in moist humus-rich soil.

In this garden, the client really wanted some drama, in order to provide a sociable space with a wow factor in which to entertain after dark. Adding electric lights instantly adds impact, while natural light, by way of lanterns, flares and candles, creates soft intrigue where it is needed. A large collection of lanterns and Moroccan wall lights are utilized at key points to maximize the mood and create a garden that really comes into its own after dark.

DESIGN ELEMENTS

This striking and characterful garden is inspired by the gardens of the Orient, Morocco and the East. Colour, water and exoticism are important ingredients, with large, verdant specimen plants adding impact and height to this north-facing space. The garden is designed to be used all year round, and be as wonderful at night as it is in the day. This is a garden for entertaining after dark; a nocturnal space, dripping with atmosphere, rich with magic, mystery and intrigue.

ABOVE *On warm evenings, lighting can transform the garden into a relaxing, leafy otherworld. Privacy is maximized by tall swathes of bamboo and an overhead shade sail, whilst the sound of water creates a tranquil filter to the sound of the city, all combining to make the lounger on the terrace irresistible.*

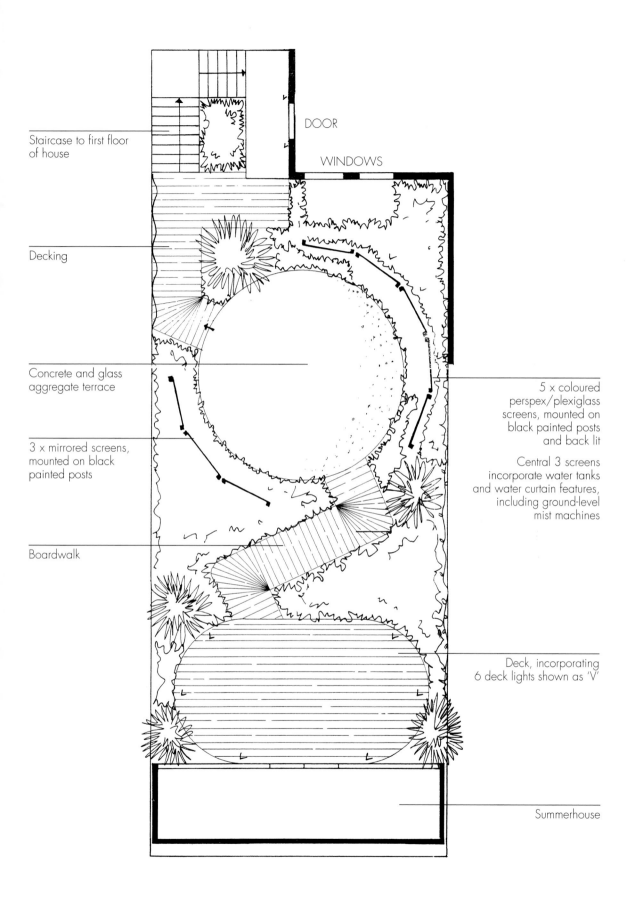

Staircase to first floor of house

DOOR

WINDOWS

Decking

Concrete and glass aggregate terrace

5 x coloured perspex/plexiglass screens, mounted on black painted posts and back lit

3 x mirrored screens, mounted on black painted posts

Central 3 screens incorporate water tanks and water curtain features, including ground-level mist machines

Boardwalk

Deck, incorporating 6 deck lights shown as 'V'

Summerhouse

WHAT YOU WILL NEED

HARD LANDSCAPING

Skip

Concrete mixer

DECKING AND BOARDWALKS

100 x 100mm (4 x 4in) pressure-treated timber posts for decking frame

100 x 50mm (4 x 2in) pressure-treated timber joists

90mm (3½in) decking frame screws

145 x 32mm (5¾ x 1¼in) treated softwood decking boards

60mm (2⅛in) decking screws – 28 screws per square metre

Concrete to support frame posts: ballast and ordinary Portland cement (5:1 ratio) plus water

CONCRETE CIRCLE

100mm (4in) uPVC strip (easily bendable)

50 x 50mm (2 x 2in) posts to support the uPVC strip, fixed with nails and road pins

100 x 50mm (4 x 2in) timber to radius length

100mm (4in) thickness of concrete: 20mm (¾in) ballast with ordinary Portland cement at 1:5 ratio

50mm (2in) depth of sharp sand, snowcrete and glass aggregate at 5:1:1 ratio with plasticizer and beige concrete additive

Mortar cleaner

WATER FEATURES

1.2m x 1.8m x 6mm (4ft x 6ft x ¼in) thick acrylic screens

2.4m x 75mm x 75mm (8ft x 3in x 3in) fenceposts

Black timber preservative to stain posts

60mm (2⅛in) stainless-steel screws

15mm (½in) copper pipe with elbow joints and miscellaneous fittings

Stainless-steel tanks: 120 x 80 x 20cm (47 x 31½ x 8in)

Steel grid cut to size to support aggregates

Coloured aggregates

Pumps

Misting machines

MIRRORS

Polished stainless-steel mirrors

2.4m x 75mm x 75mm (6¾ft x 3in x 3in) fenceposts

Black timber preservative to stain posts

60mm (2⅛in) stainless-steel screws

SHADE SAIL

5sq m (64sq ft) shade sail

Four 2.4m x 75mm x 75mm (8ft x 3in x 3in) posts

Postfix ready-mix concrete to concrete vertical support posts. One 20kg bag will fill a 30 x 30 x 30cm (12 x 12 x 12in) hole. Use 40kg of concrete per post.

Fixings

TRELLIS

Chelsea (square lattice) trellis

LIGHTING

Low voltage, black, powder-coated spike lights

Cables, clips and other accessories

Transformers

Junction boxes

Remote control

IRRIGATION

Irrigation timer

Low-pressure porous pipe

Tap connectors

Valves

Pipe pegs

NB Measure your garden carefully, in order to establish the quantities required to suit your particular outdoor space. All electrical work within gardens has to conform to building regulations, and final connection to mains power has to be done by a qualified electrician.

PLANTING

Potentilla 'Red Ace'

BEHIND PERSPEX/PLEXIGLASS SCREENS

Phyllostachys nigra

BETWEEN PERSPEX/PLEXIGLASS SCREENS

Soleirolia soleirolii

IN FRONT OF RIGHT WATER SCREEN

Equisetum hyemale

Mimulus 'Bonfire Red'

Zantedeschia aethiopica 'Crowborough'

IN FRONT OF LEFT MIRROR SCREEN

Darmera peltata

Echinacea purpurea 'Magnus'

Euphorbia griffithii 'Dixter'

Hedychium coccineum 'Tara'

Ophiopogon planiscapus 'Nigrescens'

SMALL MIXED BED

Anemone x *hybrida* 'Honorine Jobert'

Cirsium rivulare 'Atropurpureum'

Crocosmia 'Emily McKenzie'

Hedychium coccineum 'Tara'

Hemerocallis 'Lemon Bells'

Rudbeckia fulgida deamii

GROUND COVER PLANTS

Agapanthus Headbourne Hybrids

Anemanthele lessoniana

Canna sp.

Gunnera manicata

Sedum 'Autumn Joy'

Verbena bonariensis

BENEATH THE STAIRCASE

Alchemilla mollis

Blechnum spicant

Carex pendula

Lychnis flos-cuculi

Matteuccia struthiopteris

Primula bulleyana

SPECIMEN PLANTS

Dicksonia antarctica (1.5m/5ft)

Trachycarpus fortunei

CLIMBERS

Lonicera periclymenum 'Belgica'

Passiflora caerulea

Parthenocissus henryana

Trachelospermum jasminoides

Vitis coignetiae

NB *Plants are usually grouped in numbers of 3, 5 and 7, but the numbers you choose should be determined by the size of your garden.*

PLANTING PLAN

1. *Anemone* x *hybrida* 'Honorine Jobert'
2. *Cirsium rivulare* 'Atropurpureum'
3. *Crocosmia* 'Emily McKenzie'
4. *Ophiopogon planiscapus* 'Nigrescens'
5. *Rudbeckia fulgida deamii*
6. *Hemerocallis* 'Lemon Bells'
7. *Zantedeschia aethiopica* 'Crowborough'
8. *Phyllostachys nigra*
9. *Equisetum hyemale*
10. *Alchemilla mollis*
11. *Trachycarpus fortunei*, underplanted with *Mimulus* 'Bonfire Red'
12. *Gunnera manicata*
13. *Anemanthele lessoniana*
14. *Potentilla* 'Red Ace'
15. *Sedum* 'Autumn Joy'
16. *Anemanthele lessoniana*
17. *Sedum* 'Autumn Joy'
18. *Trachycarpus fortunei*
19. *Anemanthele lessoniana*
20. *Agapanthus* Headbourne Hybrids
21. *Potentilla* 'Red Ace'
22. *Anemanthele lessoniana*
23. *Potentilla* 'Red Ace'

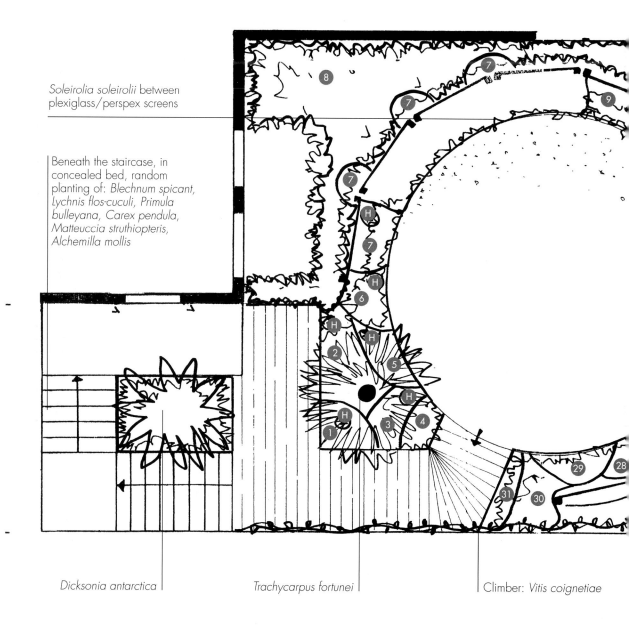

Soleirolia soleirolii between plexiglass/perspex screens

Beneath the staircase, in concealed bed, random planting of: *Blechnum spicant, Lychnis flos-cuculi, Primula bulleyana, Carex pendula, Matteuccia struthiopteris, Alchemilla mollis*

Dicksonia antarctica   *Trachycarpus fortunei*   Climber: *Vitis coignetiae*

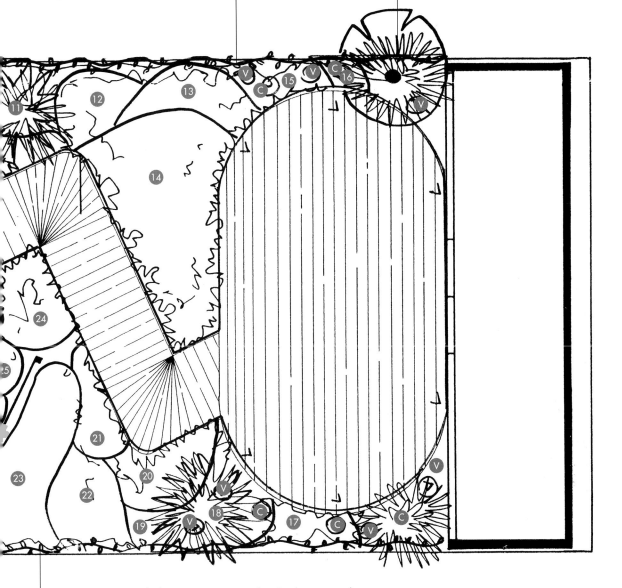

24 *Darmera peltata*

25 *Echinacea purpurea* 'Magnus'

26 *Darmera peltata*

27 *Echinacea purpurea* 'Magnus'

28 *Darmera peltata*

29 *Euphorbia griffithii* 'Dixter'

30 *Zantedeschia aethiopica* 'Crowborough'

31 *Ophiopogon planiscapus* 'Nigrescens'

H = *Hedychium coccineum* 'Tara'

C = *Canna* sp.

V = *Verbena bonariensis*

Mixed climbers:
Trachelospermum jasminoides,
Parthenocissus henryana,
Vitis coignetiae,
Passiflora caerulea,
Lonicera periclymenum 'Belgica'

Oak Tree

Mixed climbers: *Trachelospermum jasminoides, Parthenocissus henryana, Vitis coignetiae, Passiflora caerulea, Lonicera periclymenum* 'Belgica'

HARD LANDSCAPING

STAIRCASE WITH SHADY UNDERPLANTING

If you plan new staircase access into your garden, you will need to contact your local planning department. Here, plans for a structurally and aesthetically strong staircase were submitted. Specialist carpenters were employed to erect the generously proportioned staircase, and ferns and other shade-loving perennials were planted below it.

GLASS AGGREGATE SPARKLY CONCRETE

A large concrete circle at the heart of the garden provides plenty of space in which to entertain. When covered by a large shade sail, this is a particularly private space from which to enjoy all the garden components radiating out from it. Rather than the usual ballast used to mix concrete, recycled crushed glass has been added. Once laid, brushed and polished, the whole area glistens and gleams, giving character and light to this north-facing space. Its glistening effect continues after dark, reflecting the coloured electric lights.

BELOW *The crushed glass set within the concrete reflects garden lighting after dark, or shafts of dappled sunlight during daylight hours, making it sparkle beautifully.*

WATER FEATURES AND MISTERS

In order to squeeze the potential from every scrap of space, small gardens demand that vertical space is considered as much as horizontal space. Shady spaces can often be damp, but in this case water features add height while also emphasizing the garden's natural attributes. A pool or pond would take up valuable surface area, so here three upright water features satisfy as many of the senses as possible.

Three stainless-steel units filled with glass beads are placed on grills, to protect and disguise the pumps that circulate the water from the unit up through a tall copper piping framework. The water falls like a simple shower cascade from just above head height. The knockout effect of this sheet of shimmering water is accentuated by the use of back-lit, coloured acrylic sheets. The sheets bounce refracted light, in colours representing elements of earth, wind, and fire, around this screened-off area of the garden, adding theatricality and glamour, where bright blooms might have struggled to provide the same impact. To add ambience after dark, misters create a mysterious haze around the edges of the glistening glass and concrete terrace, which is at the heart of the space.

These water features definitely require professional installation, not least due to the complicated construction, but also due to regulations governing garden electrics. Operated by remote control, these water features, lights and misters can be switched on and off at whim, from anywhere in the house or garden, including from the summerhouse at the bottom of the garden.

SUMMERHOUSE

Once in the garden, traipsing through the space up the staircase to the kitchen to make a cup of tea, and then back down again, would have been particularly arduous. Therefore, the existing summerhouse at the bottom of the garden was repainted and made fully functional to accommodate outdoor living, with plumbing and electrics installed to create a fully working outdoor kitchen. Wall-mounted heaters were fitted to the outside walls to encourage outdoor living, even in the most unseasonable of temperatures.

ABOVE *Bouncing light and reflections into this small north-facing garden, mirrors are a wonderful way to create the illusion of space. Less heavy, more cost effective and safer than glass, acrylic screens are the best choice.*

SHADE SAIL

In order to provide the maximum amount of privacy and create a sun-screened space, a shade sail, whether bespoke or off-the-shelf, is a great solution. It can create a real architectural feature in the garden and can be used temporarily, then quickly folded away, or as a more permanent garden feature. They are a good alternative to the more cumbersome gazebo.

As this garden is overlooked on all four sides, an overhead shade sail adds privacy, as well as giving the space a top layer, more usually associated with the largest of trees. It is, of course, a temporary structure and can be removed easily, via a simple pulley system. When it's down, privacy is removed, but then views of the ever-changing clouds in the sky are revealed.

MIRROR PANELS

Mirrors in any small garden are brilliantly useful in creating an illusion of space. In this garden, mirrors reflect light, create privacy for the summerhouse at the end of the garden and make this small space appear twice its size. Situated opposite the water features in a shady spot, they double the effect of the water walls by making you feel as if you are surrounded by water, without going to the expense of installing the water features twice! They also bounce light into the garden, which is important in a north-facing space. Made from acrylic, which is much stronger than glass, and lighter too, the screens are easy to install, fixed to standard fence posts that are concreted into the ground.

SOFTWOOD DECK AND BOARDWALK

As the bottom of this garden faces south, and so receives the most sun, it makes sense to utilize this as a secondary seating area. Outside the summerhouse, an area of decking is reached via a directional boardwalk running through the planting. The boardwalk allows you to get up close and personal with the planting. Because it is laid diagonally through the space, the boardwalk also creates the sense of embarking on a journey and gives the illusion of additional space.

LIGHTING

Lighting is absolutely key to this garden, and amazing effects are created with simple, low-voltage, black, powder-coated spotlights in key places around the garden, in combination with Moroccan wall lights (adapted for electricity). In addition to electric lighting, copious lanterns are used to inject oceans of glamorous flickering natural light.

In this garden, black lamp fittings are ideal, as the light they exude is more important than seeing the light source itself. Black lamps tend to fade away into planting groups and behind screens, whereas brass or chrome fittings are much more obvious. Zoned in separate circuits by a qualified electrician, lights can be turned on in groups by a remote control from within the garden itself. This negates the need to chase electrical fittings into the house – an essential consideration for this garden, where access up and down stairs into the house to turn lights on and off would be very trying!

PLANTING

SPECIMEN PLANTS

DICKSONIA ANTARCTICA

Tree ferns have an alluring quality and are ideal in
this shady north-facing space. Adding height and span,
Dicksonia antarctica seems to pervade this garden.
Seen on entering from the ground floor gate, they
immediately give an impression of the glamorous excess
that lies in the garden beyond. Protected from strong,
drying winds and planted into rich, fertile soil, the tree
fern's trunk needs to be well watered. A liquid feed
applied once a month when in growth will keep the
plant looking good.

TRACHYCARPUS FORTUNEI

Evoking foreign climes, the Chusan palm, *Trachycarpus
fortunei* is the perfect plant for adding height, evergreen
interest and character to such an exciting garden.
This urban sheltered spot allows for a range of tropical
plants to be grown, and this palm is the upper storey
to underplantings of bamboo, *Zantedeschia* and
Hedychium. Mature plants, such as this, can be
extremely heavy to move around the garden, so, to save
your back, decide on final planting position before your
plant arrives. Make sure that it is planted in well
prepared fertile soil, out of direct sunshine and wind.

GROUND COVER PLANTS

SOLEIROLIA SOLEIROLII

This is the ideal plant for a damp, shady courtyard.
Soleirolia soleirolii (Baby's Tears or Mind Your Own
Business) is the perfect plant for creeping around
the terrace. Mist from the misting machines curls over
and around it, not only creating a wonderful effect,
but also on a more practical note, the water droplets
keep the plants moist. *Soleirolia soleirolii* has quick-
spreading roots, filling any awkward crevices and
gaps to marvellous effect, rather like the moss seen in
Japanese gardens.

BELOW *Towering plants envelop this small space to create
an urban oasis. The planting and colours immediately
distance you from the confines of the city, evoking other
countries and climates thousands of miles away.*

AROUND THE TERRACE

DARMERA PELTATA

A striking, architectural, herbaceous perennial, reminiscent of the huge *Gunnera mannicata*, but with more diminutive proportions, makes *Darmera peltata* suitable for the smaller garden. Lush, green leaves unfurl in spring forming almost perfect circles up to 60cm (24in) across. In autumn, the colour of the foliage changes into fiery shades of red, to provide a finale of interest, before the plant disappears below ground to hibernate during the winter months. Used around the circular terrace, the rounded foliage provides a curvy backdrop to the hard landscaping.

EQUISETUM HYEMALE

A prehistoric-looking curiosity, this fast-growing horsetail is most associated with water, and so the perfect addition to planting beside the water features. Clump-forming, this reed-like, tubular plant, with its strangely bare and banded stems, snake skyward reaching over 1m (39in) in height; it is bound to be a talking point.

METHOD

With so many elements making up the garden, the timing of deliveries into this small space will be absolutely key. You will need to ensure that you are not overrun with materials.

1 CLEARANCE AND MARK OUT

Remove everything that you don't want to keep in the garden. This can be straightforward if you have no existing hard landscaping to remove. Digging over the garden and removing all the perennial weeds can be an arduous task. However, it is necessary to do this in order to avoid weeds springing up in borders at a later date. Although organic gardening is generally the way forward, it is a good idea to use a systemic weed killer over the whole area, a week or so before the landscaping begins. It will kill all weed growth both above and below ground.

Mark out with spray line (available from builders' merchants) the layout of your new garden, including the proposed concrete circle. This is best done by placing a peg in the centre point of the area (as the whole garden radiates out from this point), then, using a piece of string stretched from the peg, mark out with canes the shape or circle that you propose. Next, spray line the edge of the shape.

2 BOUNDARIES

Hopefully, your boundary fencing will be intact. If not, now's the time to fix it. For this garden, fencing, trelliswork and walling was installed to mark out the garden's boundaries, before moving on to the internal construction. It's almost always the case that you start at the edges of your garden and work your way in.

3 CONCRETE CIRCLE

The circle's central point, and the circle itself, will be established at the marking out stage (see above). To prepare for the concrete, drive the road pins into the ground around the edge of the circle every 30cm (12in). Clamp the uPVC strip (which bends more easily than

ABOVE *A boardwalk from the central terrace leads through lower level planting to a secluded deck and garden room at the rear of the space.*

plywood) into position to form a circular support for the concrete. It is important to make sure that the uPVC is level. Then, drive the wooden pegs (50 x 50 x 500mm/2 x 2 x 19¾in) into the ground on the outside of the circle and screw the uPVC to these posts, using pozidriv 50mm (2in) woodscrews. Once the uPVC is secure, remove the road pins. Next, dig out the arc for the circle to a depth of 100mm (4in).

At the central point put a wooden peg (50 x 50 x 500mm/2 x 2 x 19¾in) in the ground. It should be 50mm (2in) higher than the outside edge to create a slope for rainwater to run down into the surrounding beds. Next, screw a length of 100 x 50mm (4 x 2in) timber to the top of this post so that it straddles the radius of the circle – use this as a guide to create a perfectly smooth finish to the final concrete surface.

Mix a layer of ordinary concrete from 20mm (¾in) ballast and cement (5:1 ratio), and fill the void (circle) halfway up to a depth of 50mm (2in). Leave the edge of the circle free of concrete – this will be filled in with the aggregate concrete, just in case the side edge is seen. Level this concrete layer and allow it to set. Then place a layer of concrete reinforcing mesh on top of the concrete to provide more support for the finished circle. Finally, mix the glass aggregate, sharp sand and snowcrete (concrete with a light colour), with the addition of a beige coloured concrete stain and a concrete plasticizer to give a good clean final finish.
Mix the sand, glass and cement dust at a ratio of 5:1:1.

Tamp (pack down) the concrete with the radial timber and use a float to ensure that you have a smooth finish. Sprinkle handfuls of glass aggregate on the surface at this (floating) stage to make sure that the concrete will sparkle once complete.

Just before the concrete is completely set, brush over it with a broom to expose the glass aggregate within. After another day, when the concrete has completely hardened, clean the surface with mortar (acid) cleaner to further enhance the glass aggregate sparkle.

4 LIGHTING AND IRRIGATION

It is always best to call upon the services of a qualified electrician to carry out the 'first fix'. Make sure that the electric cables, conduit pipes and irrigation hardware are laid in position before your paving and decks are laid. This work will be completed with the addition of lamps, cables and final pipe work when the structures, and often the planting, are in place. (See page 168 for advice on lighting.) Mulch should be added after all cabling has been completed.

5 DECKING AND BOARDWALK

Referring to your garden plan, construct the framework for the decking and the boardwalk, then lay softwood, ribbed non-slip boards on the top and screw into position. (See page 164 for advice on building a deck.)

ABOVE *Electric light supported by natural flames flickering in lanterns transforms this night garden into a sparkling otherworld after dark.*

6 STAIRCASE

At this stage the staircase needs to be put in. Specialist carpenters built this staircase on site – the last element of hard landscaping to be constructed. If this major structure is built at the beginning of the project, it may be obstructive when bringing materials in and out of the space.

7 PLANTING

Dig the beds over, adding compost and feed to all the borders (see page 176). Fit support wires to fencing or walls before planting the climbers into position. Once planted, take them off the canes and tie them on to the new support wires to ensure good, even growth. Then, place the large specimen plants in their positions. When you are happy with their location, dig deep holes, adding compost at the bottom, and plant them. Lastly, plant the smaller plants beneath.

8 FINAL ELECTRICS AND IRRIGATION, THEN MULCH

Wire the lamps up and lay the irrigation pipes before applying a mulch to all the planting beds – this not only acts as a weed suppressant, and a feed and water retainer for the plants, but also masks any unsightly irrigation pipes.

MAINTENANCE

JANUARY

Drain your irrigation lines to ensure that freezing water doesn't damage them.

Hang bird feeders to attract birds to your garden.

Insulate your outdoor tap to prevent it from freezing.

FEBRUARY

Cut back grasses in your garden, including Anemanthele lessoniana.

Plant lilies in pots to add summer scent and colour.

MARCH

Sow sweet peas against the fences to add colour and scent – Lathyrus odoratus 'Cupani' is a personal favourite.

Cut back herbaceous perennials.

If your Potentilla is beginning to look a little overgrown, prune it back rigorously at this time, cutting into old wood down to a low bud. This will encourage new growth, which will even flower this year.

APRIL

Feed Trachycarpus fortunei with a slow-release fertilizer.

Layer climbers by bending stems to touch the ground. Pin them into place with wire. Water well, and by next year you will have new plants to bulk up your fence line with bloom.

Regularly remove weeds.

MAY

Dig up unwanted sprouts of bamboo. Thin out the bamboo, removing older canes rather than young.

Plant dahlias to add to the riot of colour, and as cut flowers for the house. Dahlia 'Rip City', D. 'Hillcrest Royal' and D. 'Magenta Star' all pack a punch.

JUNE

Cannas would be a glorious addition to this garden, and can be planted now.

Keep up with the weeding.

JULY

Plant autumn-flowering bulbs such as Crocus, Colchicum and Nerine.

Deadhead borders to keep all plants blooming for as long as possible.

AUGUST

Even though the garden has irrigation installed, some plants may need extra watering in very dry weather.

SEPTEMBER

Buy or order spring-flowering bulbs, such as Muscari, Scilla and Chionodoxa, and plant them as soon as possible.

Cut back herbaceous perennials that are past their best.

OCTOBER

Because this garden is sheltered, tree ferns should not require winter protection. However, if your garden is more exposed, then now's the time to wrap your tree ferns in fleece, straw or polystyrene. Remove it in late spring when all chance of frost is over.

NOVEMBER

Plant bright tulips to extend the garden display. The more exotic varieties, the better.

DECEMBER

Clean the concrete terrace with a pressure washer. Surrounding plants will be hibernating below ground, so they will not be damaged by the spray.

TERRACED GARDEN

PLANNING THE GARDEN

Rarely is a garden completely flat, and although slopes can add interest, they can be difficult to cultivate and the garden can become tricky to walk around comfortably.

Steps and terracing are the time-honoured solution for a slope that is too steep to walk up easily. Both can be used constructively to link the whole garden together, and mark a transition between particular styles or themes within the space. Steps can be made from a wide variety of materials – they should be solidly constructed and safe, and tie in with other materials used in the garden.

In this sloping garden, to make life easier, the ground has been terraced to create different flat areas, each accessed by steps in retaining walls. This involves investing in some serious earth-moving equipment (diggers, electric wheel barrows and so forth), and using a cut-and-fill technique to level off the land. Usually, this is best left to professional landscapers. Although it is costly, terracing will certainly provide a series of eminently more useable spaces, each with their own personality or style.

DESIGN ELEMENTS

If the slope of a garden is proving difficult, for instance if you want your garden to accommodate many uses – not least to be able to walk through the space without straining your calf muscles – terracing the garden is the solution. Creating level areas with retaining walls, each space linked by steps, will allow for easy movement around the garden. In addition, the various sections can be individualized, with different styles to suit the mood, depending on the time of day and where the sun lies.

BELOW *With generous steps reaching up into each level, and each terrace retaining wall camouflaged with planting before it, a sloping garden can offer several garden rooms.*

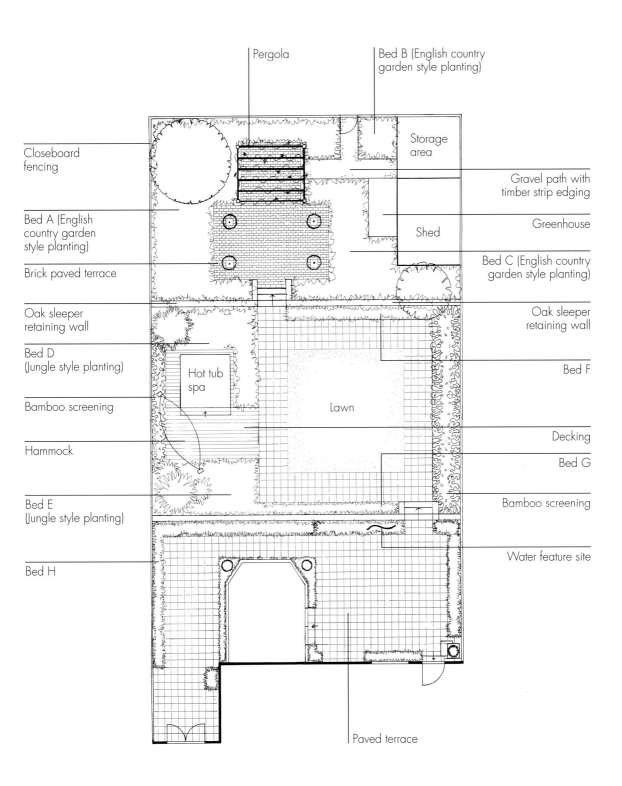

Pergola

Bed B (English country garden style planting)

Closeboard fencing

Storage area

Gravel path with timber strip edging

Greenhouse

Bed A (English country garden style planting)

Shed

Brick paved terrace

Bed C (English country garden style planting)

Oak sleeper retaining wall

Oak sleeper retaining wall

Bed D (Jungle style planting)

Hot tub spa

Bed F

Bamboo screening

Lawn

Hammock

Decking

Bed G

Bed E (Jungle style planting)

Bamboo screening

Water feature site

Bed H

Paved terrace

WHAT YOU WILL NEED

HARD LANDSCAPING

Skip

Concrete mixer

Concrete (ballast, ordinary Portland cement, water)

PAVING

MOT type 1 scalpings

Sharp sand and cement for paving

600 x 600mm (23½ x 23½in) Stonemarket truslate sage paving

Soft sand and cement mix (4:1 ratio) for pointing

RETAINING WALL

100 x 100mm (4 x 4in) treated softwood posts for supports

Concrete mix to support posts

Treated softwood railway sleepers

Steel reinforcing rods to drive through sleepers to fix together

Geotextile filter material for lining rear of wall

STEPS

100 x 100mm (4 x 4in) treated softwood posts for supports

Concrete mix to support posts

Treated softwood railway sleepers

MOT type 1 scalpings

Sharp sand and cement for paving

600 x 600mm (23½ x 23½in) Stonemarket truslate sage paving

Soft sand and cement mix (4:1 ratio) for pointing

NB Measure your garden carefully, in order to establish the quantities required to suit your particular outdoor space.

DECKING

100 x 100mm (4 x 4in) treated timber posts for decking frame

100 x 50mm (4 x 2in) treated timber joists

145 x 20mm (5¾ x ¾in) smooth Ipe hardwood

65mm (2½in) stainless-steel screws

HOT TUB SPA

Concrete base, 100mm (4in) thick

PATH AROUND LAWN

MOT type 1 scalpings

Sharp sand and cement for paving

300 x 300mm (11¾ x 11¾in) Stonemarket truslate sage paving

Soft sand and cement mix (4:1 ratio) for pointing

BRICK TERRACE

MOT type 1 scalpings

Sharp sand and cement to bed paving

Freshfield lane bricks

Kiln-dried silica sand to brush into paving joints

Stabilizing solution

PERGOLA

100 x 100mm (4 x 4in) posts

100 x 50mm (4 x 2in) bearers and joists

Concrete mix to support posts

70mm (2¾in) galvanized wood screws

PLANTING

ENGLISH COUNTRY GARDEN

BEDS A, B & C

Alchemilla mollis

Achillea 'Moonshine'

Anemanthele lessoniana

Aquilegia 'Black Barlow'

Aquilegia 'Ruby Port'

Bergenia cordifolia

Ceanothus impressus 'Puget Blue'

Cornus alba 'Aurea'

Cornus kousa chinensis 'Rubra' multistem

Crocosmia 'Lucifer'

Digitalis ferruginea

Echinacea purpurea 'Rubinstern'

Euphorbia griffithii 'Dixter'

Forsythia x intermedia 'Spectabilis'

Gaura lindheimeri

Geranium 'Johnson's Blue'

Gleditsia triacanthos 'Sunburst' (tree)

Hamamelis mollis

Helenium 'Moerheim Beauty'

Helianthus 'Lemon Queen'

Helleborus x sternii

Hemerocallis 'Stafford'

Heuchera micrantha 'Palace Purple'

Iris 'Quechee'

Knautia macedonica

Miscanthus sinensis 'Malepartus'

Monarda 'Mahogany'

Nepeta 'Six Hills Giant'

Persicaria amplexicaulis
'Atrosanguinea'

Phlomis russeliana

Salvia nemorosa 'Ostfriesland'

Salvia officinalis

Sambucus nigra 'Guincho Purple'

Sisyrinchium striatum

Stipa tenuissima

Syringa vulgaris 'Madame Antoine
Buchner'

Tellima grandiflora

Verbena bonariensis

JUNGLE BEDS D & E

Agapanthus Headbourne Hybrids

Asplenium scolopendrium

Bergenia cordifolia

Blechnum spicant

Canna varieties

Chamaerops humilis

Crocosmia 'Emberglow'

Crocosmia 'Lucifer'

Crocosmia 'Solfatare'

Darmera peltata

Deschampsia cespitosa

Dicksonia antarctica

Euphorbia mellifera

Gaura lindheimeri

Helleborus x sternii

Hosta 'White Christmas'

Luzula nivea

Musa basjoo

Persicaria filiforme

Phormium 'Yellow Wave'

Phyllostachys nigra

Rodgersia pinnata

Trachycarpus fortunei

Verbena bonariensis

BEDS F & G

Alpines and herbs, including:
Sedum acre, thyme, marjoram,
mint, etc., Hebe, Echinacea,
Penstemon

BED H

Achillea 'Feuerland'

Alchemilla mollis

Allium schoenoprasum

Aquilegia 'William Guinness'

Deschampsia cespitosa

Euphorbia amygdaloides 'Rubra'

Geranium macrorrhizum 'Bevan's
Variety'

Helenium 'Moerheim Beauty'

Helenium 'Sahin's Early Flowerer'

Helianthus 'Lemon Queen'

Hemerocallis 'Hyperion'

Hemerocallis 'Stafford'

Sedum 'Herbstfreude'

Weigela florida 'Variegata'

BAMBOO RUN

Phyllostachys nigra

PLANTING AROUND HOUSE

Aquilegia 'Black Barlow'

Geranium macrorrhizum 'Bevan's
Variety'

Helenium 'Moerheim Beauty'

Lavandula angustifolia 'Hidcote'

CLIMBERS

Clematis balearica 'Freckles'

Clematis 'The President'

Lonicera japonica 'Hall's Prolific'

Parthenocissus henryana

Passiflora caerulea

Trachelospermum jasminoides

POTS

Laurus nobilis topiary lollipops

Ligustrum delavayanum topiary
lollipops

NB Plants are usually grouped in
numbers of 3, 5 and 7, but the
numbers you choose should be
determined by the size of your
garden.

PLANTING PLAN

BED A

1. *Geranium* 'Johnson's Blue'
2. *Alchemilla mollis*
3. *Helianthus* 'Lemon Queen'

4. *Salvia officinalis*
5. *Gaura lindheimeri*
6. *Syringa vulgaris* 'Madame Antoine Buchner'
7. *Monarda* 'Mahogany'
8. *Alchemilla mollis*

9. *Aquilegia* 'Black Barlow'
10. *Iris* 'Quechee'
11. *Sambucus nigra* 'Guincho Purple'
12. *Forsythia* x *intermedia* 'Spectabilis'
13. *Knautia macedonica*

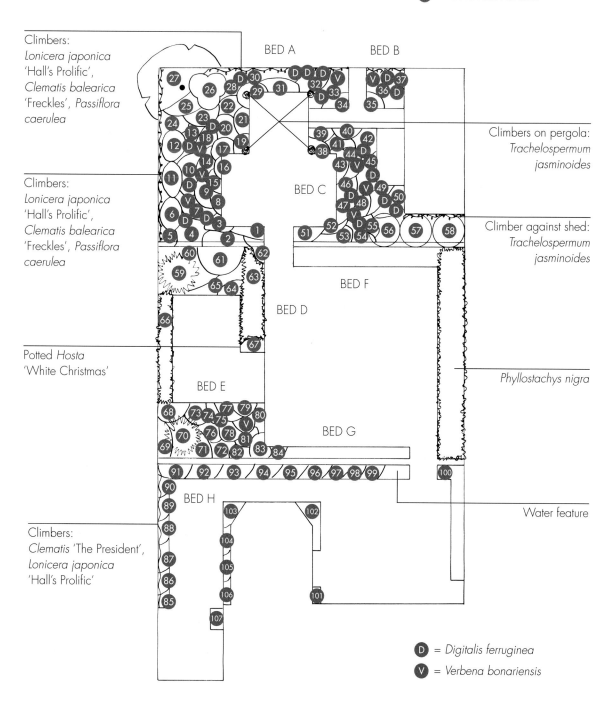

Climbers:
Lonicera japonica 'Hall's Prolific', *Clematis balearica* 'Freckles', *Passiflora caerulea*

Climbers:
Lonicera japonica 'Hall's Prolific', *Clematis balearica* 'Freckles', *Passiflora caerulea*

Potted *Hosta* 'White Christmas'

Climbers:
Clematis 'The President', *Lonicera japonica* 'Hall's Prolific'

BED A

BED B

Climbers on pergola:
Trachelospermum jasminoides

Climber against shed:
Trachelospermum jasminoides

BED C

BED F

BED D

BED E

BED G

Phyllostachys nigra

Water feature

BED H

D = *Digitalis ferruginea*

V = *Verbena bonariensis*

(14) Achillea 'Moonshine'

(15) Crocosmia 'Lucifer'

(16) Alchemilla mollis

(17) Tellima grandiflora

(18) Anemanthele lessoniana

(19) Helleborus x sternii

(20) Nepeta 'Six Hills Giant'

(21) Bergenia cordifolia

(22) Gaura lindheimeri

(23) Phlomis russeliana

(24) Helianthus 'Lemon Queen'

(25) Persicaria amplexicaulis 'Atrosanguinea'

(26) Cornus alba 'Aurea'

(27) Miscanthus sinensis 'Malepartus' (under-planting tree: Gleditsia triacanthos 'Sunburst')

(28) Echinacea purpurea 'Rubinstern'

(29) Tellima grandiflora

(30) Aquilegia 'Ruby Port'

(31) Anemanthele lessoniana

(32) Alchemilla mollis

(33) Sisyrinchium striatum

(34) Alchemilla mollis

BED B

(35) Alchemilla mollis

(36) Sisyrinchium striatum

(37) Alchemilla mollis

BED C

(38) Helleborus x sternii

(39) Euphorbia griffithii 'Dixter'

(40) Alchemilla mollis

(41) Echinacea purpurea 'Rubinstern'

(42) Aquilegia 'Ruby Port'

(43) Heuchera micrantha 'Palace Purple'

(44) Crocosmia 'Lucifer'

(45) Hemerocallis 'Stafford'

(46) Stipa tenuissima

(47) Salvia nemorosa 'Ostfriesland'

(48) Stipa tenuissima

(49) Helenium 'Moerheim Beauty'

(50) Knautia macedonica

(51) Geranium 'Johnson's Blue'

(52) Anemanthele lessoniana

(53) Helleborus x sternii

(54) Geranium 'Johnson's Blue'

(55) Stipa tenuissima

(56) Hamamelis mollis

(57) Ceanothus impressus 'Puget Blue'

(58) Cornus kousa chinensis 'Rubra' multistem

BED D

(59) Trachycarpus fortunei

(60) Rodgersia pinnata

(61) Musa basjoo

(62) Crocosmia 'Lucifer'

(63) Phormium 'Yellow Wave'

(64) Crocosmia 'Emberglow'

(65) Canna varieties

(66) Phyllostachys nigra

(67) Crocosmia 'Solfatare' and 'Emberglow' mix

BED E

(68) Darmera peltata

(69) Asplenium scolopendrium

(70) Dicksonia antarctica

(71) Euphorbia mellifera

(72) Helleborus x sternii

(73) Luzula nivea

(74) Passiflora caerulea

(75) Blechnum spicant

(76) Persicaria filiforme

(77) Canna varieties

(78) Chamaerops humilis

(79) Bergenia cordifolia

(80) Crocosmia 'Emberglow'

(81) Agapanthus Headbourne Hybrids

(82) Blechnum spicant

(83) Deschampsia cespitosa

(84) Gaura lindheimeri

BEDS F AND G

Random mixed plantings of alpines and herbs, including: Sedum acre, thyme, marjoram, mint, Hebe, Echinacea, Penstemon

BED H AND AROUND HOUSE

(85) Alchemilla mollis

(86) Hemerocallis 'Hyperion'

(87) Geranium macrorrhizum 'Bevan's Variety'

(88) Aquilegia 'William Guinness'

(89) Helenium 'Moerheim Beauty'

(90) Hemerocallis 'Stafford'

(91) Helianthus 'Lemon Queen'

(92) Helenium 'Moerheim Beauty'

(93) Achillea 'Feuerland'

(94) Helenium 'Sahin's Early Flowerer'

(95) Allium schoenoprasum

(96) Weigela florida 'Variegata'

(97) Euphorbia amygdaloides 'Rubra'

(98) Sedum 'Herbstfreude'

(99) Deschampsia cespitosa

(100) Lavandula angustifolia 'Hidcote'

(101) Lavandula angustifolia 'Hidcote'

(102) Lavandula angustifolia 'Hidcote'

(103) Lavandula angustifolia 'Hidcote'

(104) Aquilegia 'Black Barlow'

(105) Geranium macrorrhizum 'Bevan's Variety'

(106) Helenium 'Moerheim Beauty'

(107) Parthenocissus henryana

HARD LANDSCAPING

SLEEPER RETAINING WALLS

Although the slope of this garden is not exceptionally steep, it is a problem. If you have a sloping space, a levels survey will determine how best to split the garden. It will allow you to work out how high your retaining walls need to be, how many steps you should have, and how wide the final areas can be. This can be reasonably straightforward with a minor slope. Extend a piece of string (or even a straight-edged piece of timber in the tiniest of plots) horizontally from the highest point of the garden to the lowest point to create a simple cross sectional drawing. Measure the length of the string and the drop from it to the ground at the lowest point. If the thought of this sets your hair on end, then there are plenty of land surveyors, some specializing in gardens, who will be happy to carry out the job for you. And if your walls are higher than 1m (3ft), it is certainly advisable to bring in the services of a structural engineer.

You will also need to consider how levelling your garden impacts on your neighbours' land. Where a sloping fence at the boundaries may have sufficed before, once levelled, your garden will have a completely different profile from that of your neighbours – you may also have to install retaining walls to the side boundaries of your garden.

In this garden, three main areas have been created: the lower terrace for seating and entertaining; the central space for relaxing, with a lawn framed by a wide path, and linked to the spa/jungle zone; and a top tier, featuring a pergola covered with scented plants, in which to enjoy the evening sun. The top tier also houses a greenhouse for sowing annuals and cultivating tender plants, as well as a large garden workshop.

Retaining walls can be constructed from a wide range of materials – bricks, concrete block and render, stone,

BELOW *Wrapped with heavy planting, consisting primarily of evergreens, the jacuzzi area is almost completely screened. This ensures that it doesn't dominate the view from the lowest level and allows a feeling of privacy and seclusion when using the hot tub.*

and gabions to name a few. Railway sleepers can also be used – these are not only cost effective, but have a handsome, natural look. However, make sure that you buy clean sleepers that have not been treated with oil, or soaked with tar, which can seep out in hot weather, creating myriad problems. New oak sleepers are the very best but come at a cost; treated, tanalised softwood, as used here, is a good, effective alternative. The sleepers are stacked in the same way as bricks are laid, resulting in a linear look, and forming a strong and purposeful retaining wall with warm natural tones. Sleepers work wonderfully with plants, too. Here, planting beds, both in front and behind the sleeper walls, bring the garden together as whole, even though each garden area has its own look.

LOWER PAVED TERRACE

With guests in mind – as well as furniture, pots and a barbecue – a large terrace is indispensable, even in the small garden. Terraces often need to be larger than you first imagine. Here, the area immediately outside the house is almost completely given over to paving, except for a small plant border at the base of the retaining walls, which softens the hard landscaping. Once you have chosen your paving, spend some time considering the laying pattern. Here, a stack-bond pattern, laid in the same direction of the house, creates a calm, relaxing effect. If the paving had been laid diagonally it would have encouraged movement through the space out into the garden, while a stretcher-bond pattern (when the joints are staggered) would give the effect of broadening or lengthening the area. The pale colour of the paving lightens the space, and the natural material echoes the natural finish of the timbers that separate each area.

LAWN

A central lawn acts as a relaxing space on which to picnic and enjoy the sun. A permanent swathe of green at the heart of the garden, from which other planting emanates, is kept crisp by way of a path all around its periphery. Without the path, heavy foot fall would lead to a threadbare lawn. The lawn forms a perfect square, and the path around it serves as a frame, giving a choice as to which direction to move around the space. More practically, it creates a mowing strip to help with lawn maintenance. Laid slightly below the level of the lawn, a lawn mower can glide over the path without catching any hard edges, making mowing a dream job.

ABOVE Crocosmia, *New Zealand flax* (Phormium), Hosta *'White Christmas' and bananas* (Musa basjoo) *lend a tropical vibe to the hot tub area, perfect for evoking holiday spirit. All you need now are a swimming costume and a cocktail!*

HOT TUB SPA

A hot tub is a great place to relax with friends, and can be a wonderful focus at a party. Ideal for a small garden, it should be positioned in a secluded spot where you are not overlooked by your neighbours. Surround it with planting to create a pleasant environment for you to truly unwind. When filled with water and people, a hot tub can be very heavy, and a concrete base at least 100mm (4in) thick is usually required to ensure that it doesn't shift, which could damage it. Decking at the front of the hot tub not only provides a clean surface from which to get in and out of the tub, but also camouflages the concrete base that is required to support the weight of the tub. Tropical planting around, behind and in front of the area provides a wonderful view, as well as offering privacy and shelter from wind. Although it is not a particularly complex job for a professional, a registered electrician will need to install the electrics.

PERGOLA

At the top of the garden, a pergola, sited in the sunniest spot, gives height and allows some respite from the sun, as well as a terrific view of the garden cascading away from it. Enhanced by the climbing tendrils of the heavily scented climber *Trachelospermum jasminoides*, the pergola provides a place to sit and daydream, with a degree of privacy. Simple timber structures work best – a pergola is easy for the DIY enthusiast to build, and all elements are easily found in your local builders' merchant.

GREENHOUSE

A standard greenhouse, with typical dimensions of 2.4 x 1.8m (6¾ x 5¾ft), is often too large for a small garden. However, mini or lean-to greenhouses can be accommodated at the side of your shed, house or fence. They are perfect for extending your growing season, overwintering tender plants or raising seeds and cuttings.

WATER FEATURE

Water is an enchanting addition to any garden space, providing sound, movement and a focal point. In a small garden, the feature will inevitably be diminutive, but the impact it has will be huge. Small space water features can be wall mounted, or stand-alone as a self-contained sump and pump water feature. Both need a tank, be it set above or below ground. The tank holds a volume of water, which is pumped along a pipe, up, through, around or over some kind of decorative feature. Available in thousands of designs to suit all tastes and gardens – be they natural stone, metal, terracotta, or glass, as here – water features are relatively inexpensive to buy and easy to install, often arriving in kit form. They require little maintenance beside the occasional wipe down. You should also keep the water topped up – on a hot day, a lot of evaporation can occur – to avoid the pump burning out. Sited for maximum enjoyment on the terrace close to the house, this glass feature is enormously tactile and very safe.

ABOVE RIGHT *Respite from the sun is welcome in any garden, and this pergola on the top terrace will soon be clothed with a thick covering of the scented evergreen* Trachelospermum jasminoides *to create a shady spot.*

RIGHT *A stand-alone 'sump and pump' water feature is an easy way to add the sound of water to a small garden.*

PLANTING

JUNGLE

Verdant, lush and evocative, jungle planting is the ideal choice to encircle the outdoor spa. Plants towering above and around the spa provide seclusion, privacy and shelter from the elements, while their exoticism evokes other lands and the sunniest of climes, even on a damp day! A bank of black bamboo (*Phyllostachys nigra*) adds height and screening at the garden's boundary, and, when caught in the breeze, they also give sound and movement. The Chusan palm (*Trachycarpus fortunei*) gives height at the rear of the hot tub; the border is studded with lofty bananas (*Musa basjoo*); and voluptuous *Canna* species provide shade for the under planting. Creeping at ground level, the architectural plants *Phormium*, *Rodgersia pinnata* and *Darmera* all enjoy the damp, moist conditions, and the striking blooms of *Agapanthus* cut through their bold leaves. No exotic border would be complete without the prehistoric-looking tree fern, *Dicksonia antarctica*; its huge shaggy trunk gives rise to a mass of fronds 60cm (2ft) wide, each reaching up to 3m (10ft) long. All these plants should be planted into deep soil, and well cultivated with copious additions of compost and slow-release fertilizer. A thick layer of bark-chip mulch will add protection from winter frosts to most plants in the jungle zone, but less hardy plants should be given extra protection by covering and wrapping them in horticultural fleece or straw. (Some specimens can be housed in the greenhouse through the winter months.)

BAMBOO WALK

To the right of the middle terrace, a bamboo walk gives balance to the jungle garden opposite. This does not only provide a kind of symmetry and functional screening for the garden's right-hand boundary, but also creates an effective element in its own right. Walking beside a mass planting of huge bamboo challenges your sense of scale and allows for a sensory experience of its own. Enhance the effect by stripping the leaves from the lower canes, in order to enjoy their inky blackness. Caught in the wind, the bamboo bends and bows, the canes clatter and the foliage swooshes. Exquisite.

ABOVE *Young canes of* Phyllostachys nigra *quickly age from olive green to deepest black. Stripping leaves from the bottom of the canes allows this startling colouring to be fully appreciated.*

COTTAGE GARDEN

If you're a keen gardener, then a cottage garden could be for you. In this terraced space, distinctly separate areas allow for a mix in garden styles on various levels. On the top, pergola level, various shrubs, herbaceous perennials and climbers create a joyful celebration of colour, texture and scent. This border of mixed planting does require regular maintenance, but if you're enthusiastic about gardening, the weeding, deadheading and soil maintenance required is an enjoyable job. The brick terrace beneath the pergola is an ideal spot to watch your plants – have fun!

TRACHELOSPERMUM JASMINOIDES

With rich green, glossy evergreen leaves and masses of tiny, starry flowers covering the plant through the summer, to my mind *Trachelospermum jasminoides* is the perfect climber to train up pergolas, fences and walls in small gardens. The close confines of the small garden accentuate its sumptuous perfume while protecting it from cold and drying winds. Grow it in well-drained, fertile soil in full sun or partial shade, and feed regularly with a balanced fertilizer.

METHOD

1 CLEARANCE AND MARK OUT

Clearance from a sloping space can be arduous. The use of automated wheelbarrows to remove debris is helpful. To keep the site safe, temporary fencing may need to be erected at the garden's peripheries and close to the house. Mark out the layout of the new garden with spray line (available from builders' merchants).

2 CREATING THE TERRACING

Creating changes in levels is best left to the professionals – it is a specialist job for all but the most capable DIYer. Mini-diggers may need to be brought in to carry out the work, and a cut-and-fill technique used. Firstly, the topsoil must be removed, then the subsoil beneath (which is not fertile) levelled to roughly form the new surfaces. Next, build the sleeper retaining walls over compacted soil, supported by 100mm (4in) posts concreted into the ground, and rodded through with stainless-steel spikes to keep them together. Lastly, replace the fertile topsoil.

3 BOUNDARIES

After retaining the new levels within the garden, and at the peripheries, erect new fencing to enclose the garden once again.

4 PERGOLA

Mark out the post holes at each corner of the pergola, then dig them out to a depth of 800mm (31½in), packing some hardcore at the base of each hole. Next, concrete the posts into the ground, ensuring that they are vertical by using a spirit level on two sides of the post. Pack the cement down with an off-cut of timber – the level of the concrete should be just below ground level. Leave the concrete around the posts to set for at least 24 hours, before constructing the crossbeams, corner braces and rafters, using wood screws to prevent the structure from twisting in the future. Notching the beams into the braces will make the whole structure much stronger and longer lasting. There are plenty of off-the-shelf pergola kits available, should you prefer not to cut your own timber.

5 BRICK TERRACE

Next, construct the brick terrace beneath the pergola, working from the back to the front, leaving large planting pockets at the foot of each pergola post in order to plant climbers.

6 CONCRETE BASE FOR HOT TUB SPA

A spa will be difficult to install once the landscaping is completed, so lay conduit piping for the electrics before laying a concrete base for the spa to sit on. Make sure the base is fully set before bringing the spa into its final position. Ensure the spa is fully protected for the rest of your build. An electrician can connect the electrical supply at a later date.

7 DECKING

Using the concrete base as a level, lay a deck to provide a solid, clean surface from which to get in and out of the spa. This creates a step up from what will be the paved path, which creates visual interest and gives definition to the spa area.

8 WATER FEATURE

Prior to laying the paving, the electric supply to power the pump for the water feature should be installed, then a sump fitted below ground. The water feature should be added after the paving is laid to prevent any potential damage.

9 PAVING

It makes good sense to lay all of the paving at the same time. Start on the path in the centre of the garden. When laying paving, always make sure (and continually check) that the stones are square and level. The final path level on this middle level should be slightly below that of the lawn to aid mowing. After the path is completed, start work on the main terrace next to the house. (See page 163 for more information on paving.)

🔟 PLANTING

Thoroughly dig over all the beds and add compost to increase fertility, according to what is going to be planted. The next job is to erect wires for the climbers at the garden's boundaries, and then to plant them. In the borders it is easier to plant the large specimens first; they require bigger holes, and so have larger amounts of soil to be excavated. Once these are all firmly in the ground, plant the smaller plants around them. Lastly, cover the planting with a thick layer of mulch. A good tip is to plant the borders before the lawn is laid so that the bare earth space can be used as a holding area for the plant pots.

🔟 LAWN

After all works are complete, the lawn can be laid, rolled out onto well prepared soil like a carpet, and firmed. To firm the lawn, walk over boards temporarily laid on top of the green sward.

ABOVE, TOP *Low growing alpines and herbs behind the retaining wall allow more diminutive plants to be enjoyed.*

ABOVE *Evergreen planting softens level changes throughout the year.*

LEFT *Changes in level distinctly separate the jungle garden below from the English country garden above, the transition marked by a specimen topiary.*

MAINTENANCE

JANUARY

In very dry weather, water the topiary in pots on the top terrace.

Make sure bananas and tree ferns have adequate winter protection.

FEBRUARY

Mulch trees, shrubs and climbers.

Plant flowering summer bulbs in pots on the brick terrace.

MARCH

Get supports for herbaceous perennials in place before they begin to grow.

If it looks a bit shaggy, you can give your lawn its first cut.

Mend damaged areas on the lawn, reseed patches and neaten edges.

Sow hardy annuals, including sunflowers, cornflower, larkspur and sweet peas in the top tier of mixed planting.

Slugs may start to cause a problem as new growth appears. Use biological nematodes as an effective control.

APRIL

Begin watering plants in pots and containers.

Prune away any frost-damaged plant stems.

Sow herbs such as basil, mint and thyme in the greenhouse.

Mulch all borders before plants start growing.

MAY

Unwrap bananas and tree ferns after all risk of frost has gone.

Mow your lawn weekly to keep it in good condition.

Keep on top of weeds, which will be actively growing at this time.

Harden off plants in the greenhouse by leaving them outside for the warmest part of the day, building up time spent outside as temperatures rise.

Increase stocks of cannas and dahlias.

Thin out hardy annuals sown earlier in the year.

JUNE

Install water butts to collect rainwater for use in the garden.

Water plants when required.

Plant out summer bedding.

Shade the greenhouse if it is particularly hot. This will prevent plants from scorching.

JULY

Deadhead bedding plants and perennials to keep them flowering.

Feed the lawn with a quick-acting summer feed.

Plant autumn-flowering bulbs, such as colchicum, crocus and Nerine.

AUGUST

Collect seed from your favourite plants.

Mow the lawn less frequently if the weather is hot and dry.

Keep your water feature topped up in hot weather.

SEPTEMBER

Start lifting and splitting large clumps of herbaceous perennials.

After the first frosts have hit cannas and dahlias, lift the underground tubers in cold areas. In warmer areas, leave them in the ground protected with a thick layer of mulch.

OCTOBER

Wrap bananas and tree ferns in fleece, straw or polystyrene to protect them from winter frosts.

Keep your borders clear from leaves fallen from neighbouring trees.

Give the lawn its last cut.

NOVEMBER

Cut down faded herbaceous perennials.

Raise pots onto feet or bricks to allow them to drain properly during the winter.

DECEMBER

Protect your water feature pump from frost damage by storing it inside during the winter.

MINIMALIST GARDEN

PLANNING THE GARDEN

The minimalist garden is becoming increasingly popular, especially in towns and cities, where space and time are at a premium. Minimalist gardens perfectly reflect the unfussy look of modern interiors. The tranquil look of this garden, which benefits from an abundance of light, gives the illusion of space and provides a seamless transition from inside to out. Success in creating an outdoor room with pared down, simple elegance is in the detail. The well-thought-out design and construction, and the clean lines of the hard landscaping are key points. The quality and finish of paving, render and stripped-down trellis should be second to none. Unless you are completely confident in your DIY skills, always choose an accomplished landscaper to carry out the work. In this type of garden, carefully selected plants become living pieces of architecture, adding impact to the space. Seating and oversized feature planters add further visual weight. Lighting plays an important role in the minimalist garden, enabling you to create a different look in the evening – perfect for alfresco dinner parties, or for providing a lovely view after dark from inside the house, even in winter. Restraint is crucial, and the most successful contemporary gardens have a strong sense of 'less is more'.

DESIGN ELEMENTS

In this small, overlooked, north-east facing garden, the key to creating a low-maintenance, elegant, family-friendly environment in which to relax and entertain, was to maximize the space. The sunniest spot in the garden is in the top, left-hand corner, and this is where a seating area is located, together with integrated storage. In order to create as much light as possible, materials used are pale in colour or sumptuous in tone, and accessories are kept to a minimum, which further evokes a sense of space. Outdoor lighting pushes the hours spent in the garden long into the evening.

LEFT *Uncluttered and elegant, this minimalist space is almost entirely laid to deck, which has been oiled to give a sumptuous look. Built-in seating with storage, low retaining walls, which double up as impromptu perches, and architectural planting create sculptural interest. It is particularly stunning when lit at night.*

PLANTING PLAN

1. *Laurus nobilis* standard lollipops
2. *Astelia chathamica* 'Silver Spear'
3. *Buxus sempervirens* balls
4. *Buxus sempervirens* shrubs

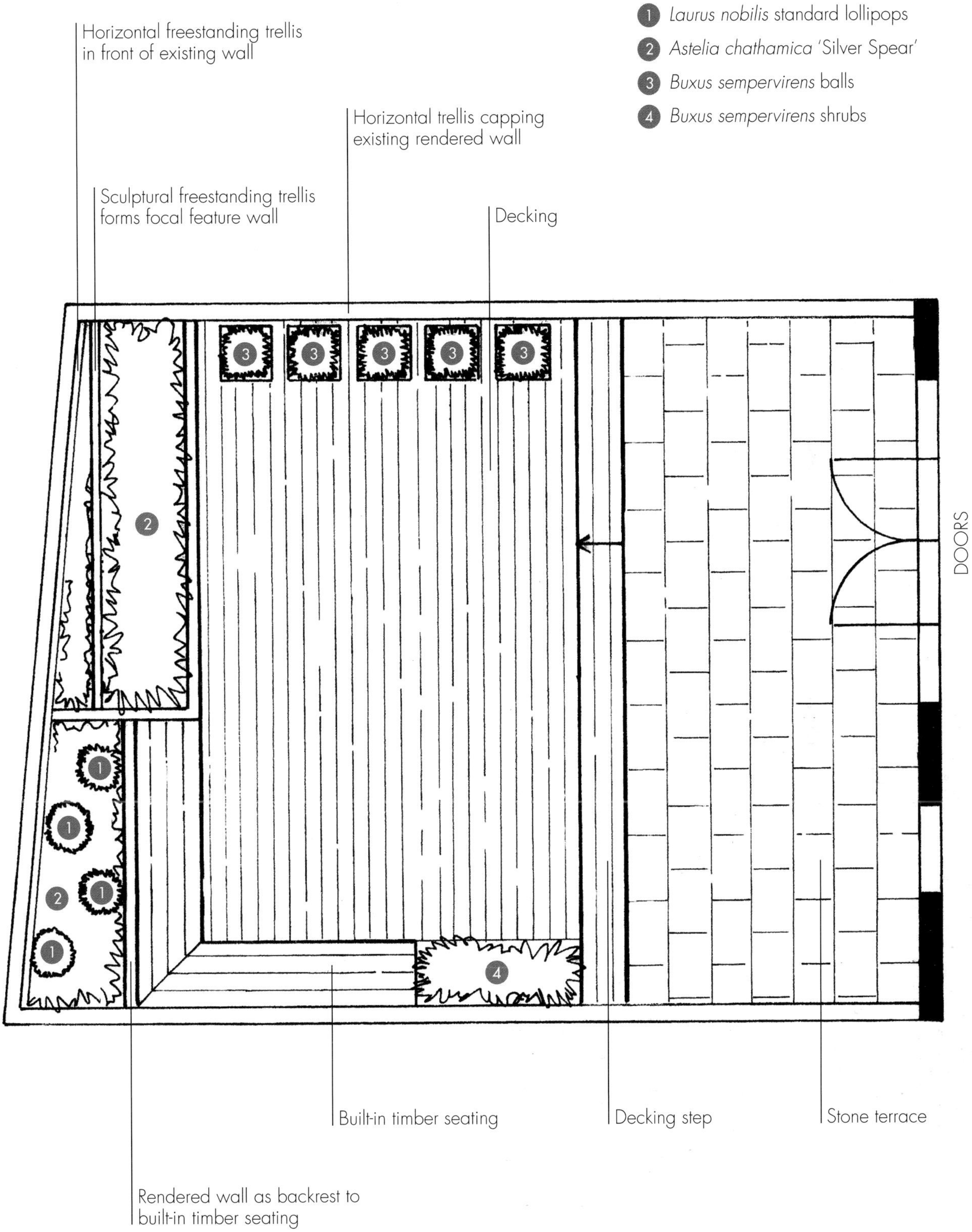

Horizontal freestanding trellis
in front of existing wall

Horizontal trellis capping
existing rendered wall

Sculptural freestanding trellis
forms focal feature wall

Decking

DOORS

Built-in timber seating

Decking step

Stone terrace

Rendered wall as backrest to
built-in timber seating

WHAT YOU WILL NEED

HARD LANDSCAPING

Skip

Concrete mixer

WALLING

Concrete for foundations

100mm- (4in-) thick solid concrete blocks

Soft sand and cement for block mortar

Stainless-steel angle beading

PVA to coat existing walling

Render applied in two coats – plasticizer, water retarder, cement, and sharp sand

Exterior masonry paint

PAVING

MOT type 1 scalpings

Aco slot drains

Access sump unit connected to existing drain gully heads

Sharp sand and cement (5:1 ratio) for mortar bed

Cava stone

Soft sand and cement mix (4:1 ratio) for pointing

Lithofin MN Stain-Stop

DECKING

100 x 100mm (4 x 4in) posts concreted into the ground

Postfix ready-mix concrete to concrete vertical support posts. One 20kg bag will fill a 30 x 30 x 30cm (12 x 12 x 12in) hole.

Use 40kg of concrete per post.

100 x 50mm (4 x 2in) joists for decking

140 x 22mm (5½ x ⅞in) smooth yellow Balau decking boards

100mm (4in) galvanized nails to secure all frameworks. Use a framing nail gun to speed up the installation process.

60mm (2⅓in) stainless-steel deck screw to fix decking to joist framework – 28 screws per metre

Decking oil

LIGHTING

Adjustable spotlights in powder-coated finish

Deck lights

Cables, clips and other accessories

Transformers

Junction boxes

Remote control

FEATURE TRELLIS

40 x 10mm (1½ x ⅜in) cedar timber

Fence posts to be resin fixed to the top of the wall

All trellis to be capped with 70 x 45mm (2¾ x 1¾in) top rail

Decking oil

IRRIGATION

Irrigation timer

Low-pressure porous pipe

Tap connectors

Solenoid valves

Pipe pegs

NB Measure your garden carefully, in order to establish the quantities required to suit your particular outdoor space. All lighting to be installed by a qualified electrician.

PLANTING

High square (polystone) planters

Polystyrene chips for drainage

Compost

Slow-release plant fertilizer

Mulch

PLANTS

Astelia chathamica 'Silver Spear'

Buxus sempervirens balls

Buxus sempervirens shrubs (50 x 50cm/12 x12in)

Laurus nobilis standard lollipops

NB Plants are usually grouped in numbers of 3, 5 and 7, but the numbers you choose should be determined by the size of your garden.

HARD LANDSCAPING

Hard landscaping is prominent in the minimalist garden, providing heavyweight permanence and structure. Here, it is architectural and ever-changing, affected by shifts in light throughout the day and as the seasons progress. It's also low-maintenance. As the space is small, using quality materials and having them installed by a professional landscape gardener, is not financially prohibitive. Excellent materials, combined with a high-end finish, ensure that, in years to come, the garden will look as good as when it was first built.

RENDERED WALLS

In order to give the space an identity, and to bounce as much light into this north-facing garden as possible, the old, deteriorating brick walls at either side have been given a coat of render and painted off-white. This makes the space seem larger than it really is, and, along with the trellis, provides a continuous boundary, enclosing the garden to form a small courtyard. Shorter internal walls, which support raised borders, are built in the same vein. They blend in with the boundary walls, establish the feeling of space and elevate the planting, making it easier to maintain. The wall on the right-hand side is just at the right height to sit on, providing further seating for larger garden parties. Rejuvenating dilapidated walls is not only a practical, cost-effective exercise, but also lends an air of luxurious sophistication to a garden.

DECK

Timber decks are a wonderful way to inject a depth of colour and a natural softness into a minimalist garden. At the same time, they perpetuate the clean lines of a contemporary space. Laid in the same way as floorboards in a house, a series of joists provide support, ventilation and extend the life of a deck. They can also be constructed over existing materials. Here, Balau decking has been chosen, not only for its rich colour, particularly when oiled as here, but also for its dense grain, overall strength and weather-resistant properties. (If not treated with oil, most decking boards will gradually age to a silver-grey colour.) Decking boards are generally available as ribbed or smooth. Ribbed boards were originally designed to provide an anti-slip finish,

and to aid rainwater runoff, although these advantages have been hotly debated over recent years. It is argued that the flat face offered by smooth boards allows water to drain away faster than grooved, and also that smooth boards are less likely to collect dirt and debris, so are easier to treat and clean. Smooth decks are, undoubtedly, much more comfortable to walk and sit on, and it cannot be denied that they offer a very contemporary look. Ultimately, selection is down to personal choice.

Laid across the garden to accentuate its width, the deck in this garden also includes two generously wide steps. Not only does this add visual interest, and a sense of 'journey' to this small space, it also allows for lighting detail to be included in the front face.

FEATURE TRELLIS

Horizontal timber trellis glides around the garden edges, further accentuating the rendered walls and clean lines of this contemporary space. Intended purely as an architectural feature, rather than a support for climbers, the trellis ties in with the deck, as it is built in the same timber. The feature trellis boundary at the rear of the garden also has a practical use. As the garden is not completely square, the deeper trellis 'wall' breaks up the render and camouflages the boundary, making it appear more symmetrical.

BUILT-IN SEATING WITH STORAGE

Seating is essential in an area of the garden that catches the evening sun. As well as providing a space-saving option, and the opportunity to include hidden storage, built-in seating reinforces the garden's design. Situated in

ABOVE *Flip lids in the benching allow for storage. Safety support arms ensure they don't slam down unexpectedly.*

the left-hand corner of the deck, the L-shaped bench adds visual interest, and can be softened with the addition of cushions. It is important to make sure that the seat is wide enough to sit on comfortably, but not so wide that you cannot lean back. These benches are long enough to lie down on, too – essential for sky gazing! Built like two boxes with flip lids, they offer excellent storage space for garden tools and children's toys, which can be tidied up and hidden away in moments. Bench storage such as this will not, however, be watertight. This can be an option with the addition of an internal storage sleeve, or a more solid timber construction, but this will add to the cost and change the look of the structure. To ensure that the lids don't slam down unexpectedly, it is sensible to include support arms with a multi-stop safety system to protect your fingers.

PAVING

A quality paving material for the lower section of the garden is made more financially attainable due to the small size of the area. Rectangles of light-attracting, crisp beige, diamond-sawn limestone are laid horizontally in order to enhance the feeling of width. In order to protect brickwork, the surface needs to have a fall away from the house, so a slot drain is included to help the water run off, without the intrusion of an ugly metal grill system.

This contemporary paving calls for minimal mortar joints between the slabs, and a colour additive has been mixed with the mortar to match the colour of the stone.

LIGHTING

The most practical effect here is the eyelid step lights that are recessed into the front edge of the steps. Primarily, these have a functional role in ensuring that the steps are properly visible. Building them into the riser (vertical) of the step, rather than the horizontal tread, means that you won't be blinded by glaring lights when walking up the steps. And a hood over the light pushes the light down, rather than across, which would be irritating when viewing the garden from within the house.

Uplights are fitted at the base of the built-in seating, and at the bottom of the tall accent planters – to invite you to sit opposite and admire them. Here, LED lights offer longevity, and ensure the light source does not become hot to the touch. A chamfered edge on the fittings protects bare feet from painful scuffing and splinters. The feature trellis behind the large raised planting bed is also uplit, to provide drama when viewed from the house, and to invite you outside to inspect the garden from close quarters.

Finally, spike spotlights within the planting beds, hidden beneath and between foliage, give a gentle glow. With a screw-lockable adjustment, these spike lights can be moved within the bed, and can also be adjusted to lock at the perfect angle to provide the most intriguing effect.

It is important to remember that all electrical work within gardens has to conform to building regulations, and a qualified electrician must fit final connections to mains power.

IRRIGATION

Watering is an essential job in any garden; even heavy rains may not provide enough moisture to keep your plants robust and healthy. If you work long hours, or don't trust yourself with the responsibility of regular watering, an irrigation system may be the answer. There are many off-the-peg systems available through the internet, builders' merchants or DIY stores; but it is sensible to consider installation at build stage, if you are to avoid cables running over areas of paving or decking. Here, a timer is attached to the existing tap, and then irrigation pipes have been threaded through conduits passing below the paving and decking, to reach all the planting beds and planters. Simple drippers disperse water to suit the plants' requirements, and, once the timer is set and running, this part of garden maintenance will never be a chore again.

PLANTING

To keep the garden simple, but full of impact, the planting is kept to a limited palette, with groups of the same species planted together. Everything is easy on the eye and very easy to maintain. Without exception, all of the plants are evergreen, ensuring that the garden is as interesting in winter as it is in summer, which is important in a tiny space.

TALL PLANT POTS

Five *Buxus sempervirens* (box) balls take on sculptural qualities when elevated and planted in tall, eye-catching, polystone pots – particularly when lit after dark. Box is extremely versatile and undemanding; it is happy in sun or shade and most soil conditions. Its foliage is extremely dense, and so is perfect for topiary.

The polystone pots are made of unsaturated resin, mixed with powdered stone additives to give a stone finish. The advantages of polystone over natural stone are more than the consideration of cost. Polystone has a sleek, contemporary look and can be moulded in different ways, allowing a greater height and variety of shape than is practical in stone. Although it has a similar appearance to stone it is much lighter, so it is extremely useful for roof gardens, where stone would be too heavy. Very smart and durable, with a uniform colour, which is not attainable with the natural texture and colour variations of stone, polystone is a perfect choice for the minimalist space. Five identically planted pots, placed side by side, add to the dramatic impact, and balance the visual weight of the seating area opposite.

BENCH HEDGE

To ensure that the hard landscaping does not completely dominate the space, a bank of *Buxus sempervirens* extend the built-in seating to break up the space. Tightly clipped to the same dimensions of the L-shaped bench, the foliage of the box becomes a glowing green architectural statement.

RAISED BEDS

Not only practical – allowing weeding and gardening to be done at waist height to save the back – the raised beds here elevate planting to provide interest at the rear

ABOVE *Clipped box continues the clean lines of the benching, simultaneously greening up the space at ground level to provide year-round interest.*

of the garden. Built around an empty central space, elements at various heights and levels (decking steps, decking, bench seats, rendered walls) hold your interest, and the clean lines and contrasting textures at the gardens periphery offer different zones to catch your eye. This results in the illusion that the garden is larger than it actually is.

ASTELIA CHATHAMICA

This is the perfect low-maintenance plant, particularly suited to north-facing gardens, and happy with the low water levels of raised beds. Additionally, *Astelia chathamica* looks wonderfully graphic when planted en masse. Arching leaves soften the straight lines of the space, and sword-like foliage reaching out from the planting beds breaks the lines of the rendered walls enclosing them. A clump-forming perennial, Silver Spear, as it is commonly known, is not completely frost resistant (especially in exposed areas), although this is not an issue in the sheltered environs of this urban courtyard. The silver, metallic bloom of the leaf makes a dramatic feature, and the leaves cast wonderful shadows against the hard landscaping.

BELOW *The rounded forms of bay topiary underplanted with a mass of silver* Astelia chathamica *contrasts with the horizontal lines of the trellis, walls and benching.*

LAURUS NOBILIS STANDARDS

Topiary standards, or lollipops, are available in various heights, and are measured by their overall height. A full-size standard has a clear stem of 180cm (5¾ft) or more, a half standard 80–100cm (2½–3ft), and there are a variety of quarter standards and mini-standards, with different sized clear stems. Here, half-standard bays have been used to elevate the eye in the rear beds, creating uplift at the back of the garden, and a strong shape and fullness that balances the large, feature trellis wall alongside this bed. Becoming living sculpture, bay's large leaves provide a foliage contrast to the under-planting of *Astelia*. They require little more care than regular watering, feeding and a light clip, once or twice through the summer months, to keep their shape.

BELOW *A row of tall tapered pots adds height and a focal point to be enjoyed from the benches opposite. Uplighting from the deck ensures they come into their own after dark.*

METHOD

Small spaces can be tremendously awkward for the landscape gardener. Even elementary garden clearance can be difficult, as unwanted materials stack up quickly, leaving little space for constructive work to begin. When you clear away the old to make way for the new, it is best to keep the number of people to a minimum, with perhaps one person clearing, while two remove the debris to the skip. This is particularly important when access in and out of the garden is through the house. Keeping a close eye on deliveries, and staging them to precisely when you need them, is also sensible as storage in a tiny space is a key consideration.

1 CLEARANCE AND MARK OUT

If access is through the house, you'll need to lay dust sheets and protective coverings inside the property before you even think of reaching for the sledge hammer. Removing large quantities of paving and walling can be a heavy, arduous job if it all has to be carried through the house, so keeping as much on site as possible is sensible. If you can, render existing walls and install decking over existing paving, with any other hardcore produced from clearance being used as a drainage core for the bottom of the raised beds. This will not only save workforce energy, but also cut costs and reduce contributions to landfill sites. Once the clearance is finished, mark the plan out on the ground using spray line (available from builders' merchants).

2 BOUNDARIES AND RAISED BEDS

If your existing brick walls have seen better days, but are still structurally sound, these, and the new internal walls for the raised beds (constructed on concrete foundations with concrete blocks), can be coated with render by professional plasterers. Paint with three coats when all construction is complete.

3 LIGHTING AND IRRIGATION

If you choose to install lighting, it is always best to call upon the services of a qualified electrician to carry out the 'first fix'. Electric cables, conduit pipes and irrigation hardware will need to be laid in position before your paving is laid.

4 DECKING

First construct the deck frame from tanalised softwood. This can be fitted over any existing paving. Once constructed and level, fix the smooth Balau boards into position, using stainless-steel decking screws, before giving it all a final sand down and a coat of oil to retain the depth of colour. (See page 164 for more information on constructing decking.)

5 BUILT-IN SEATING

Build the seating, using much the same method as the deck. Fix a large L-shaped box to the boundary walls, and top with a lid constructed to provide hidden storage within. Like the deck, this should be given a final sanding before finishing with a treatment of oil.

6 TRELLIS

Here, trellis batons were constructed off site by skilled carpenters, as there was limited space on site. The feature trellis is simply supported on posts concreted into the ground, but the wrap atop the newly rendered walls surrounding the garden needs to be considered more carefully. First, special posts, to which to fix the trellis, should be installed on top of the wall. Use posts fitted on the bottom edge with 10mm (⅜in) threaded stainless-steel bars. Drill the wall to a depth of 200mm (8in), and fix the posts into these holes using chemical cement resin. Fix the trellis to these posts at regular intervals, using stainless-steel screws. Fit a protective timber capping rail to all the horizontal trellis within the space, before oiling.

ABOVE *Raised beds make maintenance easy and raise plants closer to eye level to be better enjoyed. The wall also doubles as a backrest to the bench seats. A change in height in the lower retainer allows for an armrest and extra seating when entertaining friends.*

ABOVE *A successful minimalist garden is all about attention to detail. Every aspect of the landscaping must be millimetre perfect. Repeated topiary plants, such as these box balls, must be clipped with great precision.*

7 PAVING

The limestone pavers (which should be treated with protective Lithofin Stain-Stop) can be laid in the same way as any other paving stone, on a full mortar bed to ensure that all the slabs are wholly supported (see page 163). Make sure that a fall runs away from the house. To stop rainwater settling where the paved terrace meets the deck, install a slot drain and connect this to the existing drainage system. Once the pavers are set solid, carefully point between the slabs, using a light colour pointing mix to stop staining and to complete the contemporary look.

8 PLANTING, IRRIGATION AND FINAL ELECTRIC FIX

Prepare for planting by incorporating plenty of compost and food into all the beds. Move the pots into position. Leave a drainage layer of gravel at the base of the pots, then fill with compost to just below the lip. All the plants should be planted before the lighting and irrigation drippers are installed (they should run up the back of the pots so they cannot be seen). Lastly, cover the soil with a bark-chip mulch to camouflage pipe work, retain water and suppress weeds.

MAINTENANCE

Even the most low-maintenance of spaces requires some looking after. Although it is not necessary to carry out all of these jobs each year, this section will provide a guide on what to look out for.

JANUARY

Ensure that all irrigation lines are drained to prevent freezing water from damaging them.

FEBRUARY

Service your lighting system, replacing wiring, bulbs or lamps if required.

MARCH

Sweep up spent foliage that has dropped from surrounding gardens.

APRIL

Turn on your irrigation system when plants begin actively growing.

MAY

Feed all plants with a slow-release fertilizer.

JUNE

Remove all dead, damaged or diseased foliage from your plants.

Give all topiary pieces a light cut in order to keep them in shape.

JULY

Top up bark-chip mulch in the borders.

AUGUST

Midway through the season, it is a good idea to pressure wash your paving to remove ingrained dirt and algae, and to keep it looking good.

SEPTEMBER

If necessary, re-oil your deck while the weather is still dry.

OCTOBER

Clean and store away additional garden furniture, if you don't intend to use it through the winter.

NOVEMBER

Continue brushing up fallen leaves that stray into the space from surrounding gardens.

DECEMBER

Turn off your irrigation system while plants are dormant. Remove the timer, to protect it against winter weather.

TECHNIQUES

HARD LANDSCAPING

Hard landscaping comprises all the surfacing, structures and paved areas that provide a garden's blueprint, alongside soft landscaping, which refers to soil preparation and all planting elements. Although a variety of materials were used to construct the gardens in this book, the methods used to form the hard landscaping element of the gardens were the same, or very similar. These 'how to' pages are designed to provide a guide in basic landscaping techniques, with a further reading list (see page 191) to give more in-depth information.

HOW TO LAY A PAVED AREA

1 Before you begin, mark lines on timber pegs to indicate the finished depth of your hardcore layer, bedding mortar and final surface layer of your paving. This will act as a guide when digging out your patio area, and when installing foundations and so forth. Next, mark out the outline of your terrace with pegs, which should be hammered into the ground so that the tops of the pegs are at final paving level. Use string or spray line (available from builders' merchants and garden centres) to define the outline. Remember to allow a minimal fall away from the house to allow rainwater to drain away into the garden. *NB When a patio is built next to a house, the final surface level of the paving must be at least 150mm (6in) below the damp proof course.*

2 Excavate the area to a depth of around 150mm (6in) to allow for foundations, mortar bed and paving layer.

3 Add a layer of hardcore (hardcore will need to be covered with sharp sand to fill any gaps), or MOT type 1 scalpings to a depth of 100mm (4in) over the whole area. Rake it out evenly, then compress the hardcore to form a solid base. It's best to hire a vibrating plate compacter to do this job.

4 Hire a concrete mixer to create a bedding mix of sharp sand and cement in a ratio of between 4 or 5 shovels of sand to 1 of cement. This can be applied semi-dry or wet for standard slabs. Add water sparingly to suit your preference.

5 Put down enough bedding mix, at a depth of 25–45mm (1–1¾in), to lay your slabs one at a time.

6 Use a builders' square to check that your paving line is square to the house, then lay your first slab against the house. Use a string line as a guide to keep everything in line. Gently tap the slab into position with a rubber mallet, using a spirit level to check your levels, and continue with this method until all slabs are laid. Use 10mm (⅜in) spacers in all the joints to ensure the jointing gaps between slabs are all the same size.

7 Once laid, leave your bedding mortar to set overnight before pointing the gaps in between your paving. Make up a semi-dry mix of mortar in a cement mixer using 4 parts of soft sand to 1 of cement, plus a small amount of water. Remove your spacers and then use a pointing trowel to press the mortar into the gaps between your slabs. Leave to dry and then brush off the surplus. To ensure slabs do not stain, and also to set the mortar joints, wash the slabs off with a clean damp sponge to remove any missed excess cement.

8 Leave the mortar to dry out completely before using your terrace.

9 A sealant can be used over natural stone to protect your terrace from stains and spills, although do be aware that this may affect the colour of the paving material.

TIP If you are planning to add lighting or irrigation to your garden, ensure that conduit runs are in position underground before you lay your terrace.

LEFT *Sweeping curves in hard landscaping are best achieved with small modular paving. Here mixed setts add texture and movement to a small space.*

HOW TO BUILD A DECK

1 Use a piece of graph paper to plan the layout of your deck before you start construction. This will ascertain the correct positioning of the upright support posts, and the length of your joists and boards. If accurate it will also act as a timber-cutting list.

2 Concrete 100 x 100mm (4 x 4in) timber posts – the main support for the decking frame – into the ground to a depth of 500mm (20in), at roughly 1.2m (4ft) intervals. Shape the top of the concrete so that it slopes away from the post. Once installed, cut the posts to the required height and then treat the cut end with an end-grain preserver. In certain garden areas, upright support posts may not be necessary; for example, if you are paving over an existing level span of paving materials. If this is the case, rather than fixing joists to upright posts, the deck frame joists can sit directly on top of levelling plastic packers, or concrete pads, which will allow air to circulate around the timber.

3 If fixing your deck to a wall (or house), attach a joist beam to the wall using expanding masonry bolts and washers, alternating holes at the top and bottom of the joist along its length. Joists running away from the wall (or house) will be attached to the joist beam at frame-building stage by using joist hangers at their end.

4 Cover the ground below your deck with a weed-proof membrane held into position with gravel or membrane pegs.

5 Next, construct your deck sub-frame. Cut the outer joist to the correct length, allowing for a timber overlap at the corners. Use 100 x 50mm (4 x 2in) fully treated softwood timber for the joists, fixing them in position to the upright foundation posts using coated coach bolts or adequate screws.

6 Decide on which direction you want the decking boards to run, then lay the inner joists in the opposite direction – allowing no more than 400mm (15¾in) between joists. Fix them with galvanized nails, stainless-steel screws or coach screws through the outer frame and into the end of each inner joist.

7 Lay the decking boards across the sub-frame so that they uniformly overlap the frame end. If your deck is particularly large you may need to lay boards end to end; make sure that the joins are positioned on top of a joist and that the join is staggered when the next row of boards is laid. Leave a gap between boards of roughly 3mm (⅛in) to allow air to circulate, water to drain away and for the boards to expand and contract according to the weather. Deck screws provide a good general spacer; they can be wedged between boards as they are laid and removed later.

8 Fix each board to the sub-frame, using 50 or 60mm (2–2⅓in) deck screws, spaced evenly.

9 Finally, if you haven't already cut the boards to length as they were being laid, use a jigsaw to cut the boards. Treat the cut ends with an end-grain preserver.

RIGHT *Decking is available in a host of different materials. Hard woods have greater longevity than soft. Green oak looks wonderful in this rural garden.*

BELOW *The direction that deck boards are laid can create the illusion of additional width or length. Joints can also be laid to draw your eye to an attractive view.*

HOW TO BUILD A PANEL FENCE

Essentially there are two main types of fencing available on the market today. Firstly, there are larch-lap and woven panels. These offer value for money, are easy to erect and are available in various heights between 90cm (3ft) and 180cm (6ft) high. Secondly, there is closeboard fencing, which is constructed entirely on site. Closeboard fencing comprises of featheredge boards that are nailed onto arris rails secured to posts. Recently, closeboard *panels* have become available – these give the look of closeboard fencing in a ready-made panel. They are erected in the same way as larch-lap and woven panels, as described below. Alternative options include picket fencing, hazel panels, palisade and trellis panels, all of which are erected in much the same way.

1 If you need to replace a fence, check your property deeds to see which boundary line belongs to you. It is best to discuss plans for fencing with your neighbours before you go ahead with your plans. Unless your boundary meets a public highway, you will usually not need planning permission for a fence less than 60cm (2ft) high.

2 Remove old fencing, unwanted climbers and weeds, then level the ground.

3 Calculate the length of the posts according to the overall height of your fence. You will need posts long enough to accommodate the panel, a gravel board, and an extra 60cm (23in) to concrete below ground. A gravel board fitted under the fence panel between the posts is not essential, but will stop soil damaging the panel itself – gravel boards are much cheaper to replace than a complete panel. They are usually pressure-treated sawn timber, but are available in concrete too. The standard size tends to be 22mm (1in) thick, 183cm (6ft) long and 150mm (6in) deep. Fence posts are available in various lengths in timber or concrete. Although timber looks softer in a garden environment and is easier to install, concrete is a longer-lasting option. Posts are available in 75 x 75mm (3 x 3in) or 100 x 100mm (4 x 4in); personally, I find the wider posts give a more professional look.

4 Careful measuring of the boundary line is essential to determine the position of the posts. Stretch a 30-metre (98½ft) tape measure firmly on the ground along the proposed fence line and mark out where the posts will go. Alternatively, you can use a fence panel to mark the positions. To save your back, use a wooden batten cut to the same length of the panels as a guide, then dig your first post hole. A width of just over the width of a spade will allow you to pack concrete into your hole around your post, and a standard depth of 450mm (17¾in) is usually deep enough. In soft ground,

ABOVE *Bespoke hardwood trellis may not be the cheapest option, but it will add individuality, quality and longevity to your outdoor space.*

OPPOSITE *Boundary fencing is such an obvious element in any garden, especially when first installed. It's worth shopping long and hard for panels that you really like.*

deeper holes, and subsequently longer posts, may be required. Add a thin layer of hardcore – 50mm (2in) is sufficient – at the base of your hole before positioning your fence post in the middle of the hole. Drive two short stakes into the ground at either side of the hole, then use a spirit level to check that the post is completely upright. Temporarily nail batons to the stakes and the posts to hold them firmly in position while the concrete sets.

Mix the concrete, using a ratio of 5 parts ballast (ready-mixed sand and aggregate) to 1 part cement. (Premixed bags of postcrete or ready-mix concrete are available if you prefer, but cost slightly more.) Add the concrete into your hole, to just below ground level, and slope the concrete away from the posts to allow water to drain away. The concrete can be applied dry, packed in firmly using a piece of off-cut timber, and given a light watering to assist natural groundwater, which will filter into the concrete and aid setting.

5 As is often the case, if your fence runs up to a house, fix your first post to the wall with three expanding masonry bolts, checking first that it is upright by using a spirit level.

6 It is a good idea to erect all the posts before adding the panels, to allow time for each post hole to set. Erect all of the posts as above until the complete run is in place. Unless you are using fast-setting concrete, leave them overnight to allow the concrete to set.

7 It is important that the panels do not touch the ground, either by using gravel boards, or by leaving a slight gap under each panel. If using boards, these need to be fixed into position at this point, either by packing out fence panel clips (these will be wider than the gravel boards), or other timber brackets. Attach fence panel clips to the posts evenly, ensuring that they are in line. You will need 6 clips per panel for a 180cm (6ft) fence. Lift your panel into position and then screw the panels to the posts through the fence clips.

8 Once all the panels are in position, if necessary, trim the tops of the posts so that they are all the same size. Then screw a post cap to the top of each post to protect the wood. Soaking post caps in water for a while before you fix them will stop the caps from splitting.

INSTALLING AN IRRIGATION SYSTEM

Irrigation systems take water from a tap and, via a network of pipes, pump it around the garden. They can be operated manually, or, more commonly, automatically. Irrigation certainly takes the effort and responsibility of watering the garden away from the owner, ensuring that plants are watered evenly throughout the season. Automatic systems can also water your garden if you are away from home. For larger gardens, it is worth employing the services of a professional landscaper, but there are many off-the-peg systems available from garden centres, which are easy to install in a small space.

Firstly, you will need an outdoor water supply. Your tap will need to be fitted with a battery-powered timer that turns water on and off automatically. It is worth using a multiway tap connector on your tap, to allow the use of both a hose and a water timer. A pressure connector attached to the tap will control the mains water pressure to best suit your irrigation system. A simple soaker hosepipe can be fitted to the tap, or a more efficient sprinkler/dripper system can be used. Pipelines run from the tap connection around the garden, with elbows, joints and other fixings to allow spurs, corner navigation and lengths of pipe to be connected together. Thinner micro-pipe runs from this supply tube straight to where your plants need the water most, and drippers, micro jets and mini sprinklers are fixed to this.

LIGHTING

On the whole, there are two types of exterior lighting: mains (or 240-volt) systems and 12-volt lighting systems. If you decide you need the power of a 240-volt system, a qualified electrician should be employed to carry out the work. The scale of lighting is governed by the size of the elements (planting borders/trees/structures) that you want to light up. In the largest of gardens, where mature trees abound, 240-volt power may be warranted, but for most spaces, especially small town gardens, a 12-volt system is sufficient. Low-voltage systems are the simplest and easiest to install, and the lights are run via a 12-volt transformer, which is plugged into a weather-proof socket. Cables run from transformers around the garden to the light fittings, which are often on spikes, so they can be simply pushed into the ground where lighting is required. Cables for low-voltage light fittings can simply

be laid on or just below soil level, but to avoid accidentally cutting through the cable with a spade while gardening, it is advisable to bury cables at a depth of roughly 500mm (19¾in).

There are many off-the-peg lighting systems available from garden centres and DIY stores, but if you have any doubts when installing lighting, always contact a suitably qualified electrician.

Another way of introducing lighting and extending your garden usage after dark, with a minimum of effort, is by using solar lighting. Solar cell and LED technology has improved considerably in recent years, and the design of solar lighting units has produced far superior light fittings. Solar lights have several advantages over electric light; they are environmentally friendly, can be placed almost anywhere (providing they receive a reasonable amount of sun), require no wiring and are affordable, too. During the day a solar panel uses the power of the sun to charge an internal NiCad battery, which later releases the charge to power the light. Many lights now have adjustable panels to ensure that they collect as much light as possible, even during overcast or cloudy days. A photo-resistor cell within the light housing is sensitive to light levels, and turns the lights on automatically after dark.

Natural light is perhaps the most user-friendly form of lighting in the garden after dark, creating romance and atmosphere through natural flickering flame. Nightlights and lanterns can be sited at key positions around the garden and on the tables too. Garden flares and oil-burning torches can be driven into soil in planting borders, or in pots or buckets filled with sand. Using citronella oil in oil burning torches will also help to keep mosquitoes, gnats and midges away.

RIGHT *Garden accessories can make or break the overall look of your newly designed space, so furniture, pots and even lanterns should be considered carefully.*

FOLLOWING PAGE *Here a host of cracked-glass lanterns have been added to borders, paths and terrace to add a human element to the permanent electric lighting, and to give an eastern flavour to the space.*

PLANNING

HOW TO PREPARE SOIL FOR PLANTING

Digging improves a soil's structure, making it easier for plants to grow. It also allows you to add compost and fertilizer into the earth to provide all the food a plant needs.

When creating a flower border for the first time, double digging (lifting and turning the topsoil two spades deep) gives you the chance to cultivate the soil. It will be hard work, but will pay dividends. Digging is physically easier if you use a sharpened, quality stainless-steel spade to lift and turn the soil; a fork will loosen the ground, but it won't lift it.

It's best to dig over the ground in the autumn, especially if your garden has heavy ground. Frost and snow over winter will help break up large clods of earth, adding organic matter, sand or grit as required, depending upon your soil type.

Always wear sturdy boots when digging – they will protect your feet and give you the extra help needed to guide your spade firmly into the ground, which will make your job so much easier.

UNDERSTAND YOUR SOIL TYPE

It might be obvious to you that your soil isn't the best in the world, but the earth in your garden can be transformed with an investment of time and effort. Before you attempt to grow anything in your garden, it's best to identify what type of soil you have, as this will determine what kinds of plants you'll be able to grow.

Clay in soil means that ground will be heavy, difficult to dig, waterlogged in winter and, possibly, smelly, too. Clay is cold, and slow to warm up in spring. It is slippery and slimy when wet and sets rock hard after a dry summer spell. Roll a handful of soil about in your

LEFT *Consider the seasons when planting a border to ensure that you have interest throughout the year.*

hands; if you can shape it into a cigar shape and it holds, then you've got clay. Despite being initially difficult to work, there are several advantages to clay; it is extremely fertile, and can be improved by digging borders over and incorporating plenty of well-rotted manure, compost or lime. Coarse sand or gravel will open the soil up, making it easier to drain.

Sand in soil makes it light, free-draining and very crumbly. Water vanishes through it almost immediately, taking with it valuable nutrients; feeding and watering is needed regularly. It warms up quickly in spring and is very easy to work. This 'hungry' soil is easily improved with the addition of lots of compost or well-rotted manure (known as 'organic matter'); these particles act as miniature sponges, improving the ground's water and nutrient-holding capacities.

Chalk is usually a very shallow soil, which is free-draining and alkaline, and because water drains from it relatively easily, it only has moderate fertility. It's very light in colour and often has actual lumps of chalk in it, making it easy to identify. Adding organic matter is the best way to improve a chalky soil, but, as organic matter tends to decompose quickly in alkaline soils, it needs topping up regularly.

Loam is the ideal garden soil; crumbly and naturally moist, it has a good structure, with plenty of earthworms, it drains well and is full of nutrients.

ACID OR ALKALINE?

The pH of your garden is another indicator of what plants will, and won't, grow happily in your garden. The pH of your garden will be within a scale ranging from 1 to 14. You can establish your garden's pH by using a simple soil-testing kit available from garden centres. A pH below 7 indicates that you have an acid soil, which will support acid-loving plants, such as rhododendrons, azaleas and camellias; while a pH above 7 indicates an alkaline soil, which is a typically dry, well-draining soil that suits a wide range of perennials, such as *Eryngium*, *Verbascum* and *Pulsatilla*. Neutral soil has a pH of 7, which will support a wide range of plants.

DRAWING PLANS AND DEVELOPING DESIGNS

If you've decided to redesign your garden, then you will almost certainly have some idea of what you'd like it to look like. But before you launch into drawing plans of your existing garden, you should first of all develop your ideas by grabbing a notebook and letting your mind wander. Consider what your garden will be used for. Do you want to use your outdoor space to relax, entertain, kick a football around, as well as growing some plants? Is your preference for contemporary spaces or for softer rural influences? Do you want to include any kind of structures, such as pergolas, arbours or even a garden office? And don't forget about the practical necessities too. A washing line, bin store or shed may seem like mundane considerations at this stage, but if they will go on to be important factors in your finished garden then it is essential to include them in your early planning. Books, magazines and photos of other gardens can inspire you, refine your personal garden style and help you to narrow down your list of requirements. Let your mind run free, including likes and dislikes. Don't worry if your list includes far more elements than you could ever hope to squeeze into your space, it can be edited later. A survey of your garden will reveal what is actually achievable, as well as what is wise to include or omit.

Now, back to the drawing board. A 'to scale' plan of your garden is essential in creating a strong design that will ensure your essential garden elements – seating areas, paths, lawn and so on – fit comfortably into your space and that the cost of the garden is within your budget. You may already have a garden plan drawn up in anticipation of other alterations to your property. It's also worth checking your property's deeds, as they may well include a garden survey. Land and garden surveyors can be employed to ensure that all dimensions taken are accurate. But if you feel confident and your space is small, why not measure it up yourself using a clipboard and tape measure?

Once you've taken accurate dimensions (stopping to check and recheck measurements as you go), draw up your existing site plan on a piece of plain or graph paper. You will need to use some type of scale; perhaps the easiest is one metre to one centimetre. Include as

LEFT A thorough plan focusses your thoughts and allows you to keep track of the materials and plant quantities.

much peripheral information on your plan as you feel is necessary to facilitate your new design. Besides the obvious boundary lines, it's helpful to consider where the good and bad views are in the garden, areas which get most sun or shade, plants that you want to keep and any slopes or changes in level. Don't add anything to the plan that you are not going to keep – why bother? Additions of this kind will simply confuse you.

As regards plants, check whether your soil is acid or alkaline (see page 173). If you're unfamiliar with the ground, dig some test holes in various spots of the garden to see if you'll be gardening on clay or sand, or if the soil is badly drained. If you have mature trees, it's wise to check whether they have attached Tree Preservation Orders, or whether your garden is in a conservation area. Remember also to make sure that all your landscaping comes within your local council's planning regulations and laws.

Once drawn up, your survey plan will show the dynamics of your garden, and will help you to visualise its full potential. Put a piece of tracing paper over your outline plan, or simply photocopy it several times, and start plotting elements such as patios, paths, screens and other features. Just keep scribbling until you find an arrangement that looks good but is still practical. You could use the plans from the pages of this book and simply extend, shrink or adapt areas to the proportions of your own garden. Always ensure that paths are wide enough: 90cm (35in) for a one-person path; 120cm (47in) for a two-person path. Also make sure that terraces are large enough to accommodate tables and chairs before drawing up your final garden design. This drawing will become a blueprint to work from when deciding what you'll need and where to place everything, as well as giving you confidence and inspiration to begin your garden makeover.

Choose plants that are appropriate for their position and soil, and those that won't dominate your space when they have grown to their mature size. If your budget doesn't reach to instantly mature plants, give your young plants space, mulches such as bark chip, well-rotted farmyard manure or mushroom compost. These give a professional finish to bare earth, slow water evaporation, and reduce weeds and rot, which in turn helps your plants to grow.

MAKING COMPOST

With so much importance resting on soil improvement, if you want a great looking garden, it's madness not to make your own compost. Kitchen and garden waste is piled up to form a heap, and, about a year later, rich, crumbly compost is produced. Buy a compost bin, or make your own with some stout stakes wrapped with chicken wire and then start piling it in – it's completely free.

Besides grass clippings, all your garden waste can be added to the heap, although small branches should be chipped before they're included. Annual weeds (chickweed, groundsel, nettles) can be added without worry, providing they aren't smothered in seed, but perennial weeds should only be added at the centre of a very 'hot' compost heap (see following paragraph). Lots of kitchen waste can be incorporated, providing it has not been cooked; fruit, vegetables, teabags, eggshells and coffee grounds are all ideal. Do not add bones, meat or fat because these will attract rats. Paper, cardboard and egg boxes can be added but must be well shredded first.

Make sure that you mix up the layers of material, adding lots of dry material (dry leaves, grass and straw) to the heap and turn the whole thing at least once. Mixing and turning adds air, which is essential for the decomposition process. The compost heap will generate heat to speed the process up. In the small urban garden, where a homemade compost bin may not be large enough to produce enough heat, an insulated manufactured composter is the best way to encourage decomposition. Finally, an activator will also speed things up. Sulphate of ammonia, nettles and even urine are all good activators.

Wormeries are ready-made bins suitable for the small urban garden; a colony of worms breaks down kitchen waste in an extremely clean, efficient process to produce small amounts of compost and wonderful plant food too.

HOW TO PREPARE A CONTAINER FOR PLANTING

1 To prevent pests and diseases infecting your new display, first make sure that your container is clean.

2 Whether your container is new or a recycled object, a hole to allow excess water to drain away is absolutely essential. Use a drill to add holes to the bottom of your pot if there aren't any. If your pot is terracotta, or the plants you want to grow enjoy moist conditions, it's a good idea to line your pot with a plastic bag at this point to help retain water and so cut down on watering. Make sure that you cut several holes in the bag, particularly over the drainage hole to prevent waterlogging.

3 Next cover the drainage hole area with old pieces of crockery, to help the excess water escape.

4 Provide a drainage reservoir by adding a layer of gravel to the bottom of the pot. Roughly a tenth of the depth of the pot is adequate.

5 Now add compost to an inch or two from the top of your pot. The type of compost you use will depend on the type of soil your plants prefer. Succulents and Mediterranean plants will benefit from incorporating some grit to provide sharp drainage, while acid-loving plants, such as azaleas need ericaceous compost. Never use garden soil; it may contain weed seeds, compacts easily when watered frequently, dries out quickly and hampers root growth.

6 Mix some slow-release fertilizer (fish, blood and bone is ideal), and some swell gel into your compost. Swell gels are water-retaining granules that increase dramatically in size when watered, and then release water back when your plants need it most.

7 Add your plants, firming the compost around them, not only to insure they are well grounded but also to knock out any air pockets from the compost.

8 Add mulch to the surface of the container, leaving at least 9mm (½in) from the top so that water doesn't simply spill out over the pot's edge. A layer of gravel, glass chippings or cobbles will not only give a polished finish, but will also help prevent water evaporation and stop weeds from seeding so easily.

9 Move your plant into position, putting pot feet (pieces of wood or brick) beneath the pot so that water can drain away from it. If you group your pots together, they will be easier to water. Grouped pots also lose less water; if you're going on holiday gather yours together in a shady spot.

10 Once planted, make sure that your plant is well watered; a container can dry out very quickly in the sun and wind. If you've provided good drainage it's difficult to over water a potted plant. As a rule, most will need watering at least once a day throughout the summer.

EMPLOYING A GARDEN DESIGNER

Most people wouldn't dream of building a house without consulting an architect. If you don't have the time, inspiration or confidence to design a garden that will best suit your needs, then employing a garden designer is the best way of achieving a cohesive, attractive garden space to suit your budget. A good designer will have a wide scope of experience to draw upon in order to offer impartial advice on design, plants, hard landscaping and build costs. They should be able to create a space that will work for you and work within its environment.

A personal recommendation is a very good way of finding a garden designer. Friends and family who have recently used the services of a garden designer may be able to recommend someone. They will let you know what's involved in the process, advise you on costs and, crucially, show you their finished garden. Otherwise, gardening magazines, such as The Royal Horticultural Society's *The Garden*, or *Gardens Illustrated* can be particularly useful in your search. Both regularly include designer profiles, combined with fantastic photography, so that you can see a designer's work laid out in front of you. If nothing appeals, you can find the names of designers from Internet sites, the *Yellow Pages* or from professional organizations, such as the Society of Garden Designers (which also publishes a magazine).

Once you have identified possible designers, check out their websites and give them a call. Discuss their work and ethos, establish their fee structure, ask about their credentials, and then outline your own aspirations. Tell them your budget, but be realistic – even the most talented designer will struggle to do your garden justice if your budget is too low. The Society of Chartered Surveyors estimates that a well-designed garden can add up to 10 per cent on your property's value. In the long run, it will be worth the investment to create a space that will continue to work for you in years to come.

Preparation is essential before your first meeting. Consider what the garden of your dreams would include. This will help your designer to lock into your aspirations, while helping you to focus. Think about

your garden in the same way as you would a room in your house; tear pages from magazines, collect samples, photos, or write notes to really make the most of your first meeting. Would you like a slick landscape of steel, glass or polished concrete, or a more romantic natural landscape where plants take centre stage? Is a water feature essential, and do you want a large terrace with lighting for evening soirées? It is inevitable that whatever your desires, your garden designer will have plenty more ideas of his or her own. So, during your meeting, familiarize yourself with the designer's work; look through his or her portfolio, examining the quality of the drawings, photographs and most of all the style. If possible, visit gardens that the designer has created. Remember that every designer's work is individual, so it's important to feel comfortable with your chosen designer, and confident that their approach will work for you.

Speak to designers about their design costs, bearing in mind that design is almost always charged completely separately from construction costs. Fees may vary from designer to designer, and can be charged in different ways. Examples include an hourly or daily rate, a fixed percentage of the total contract value, or an agreed fixed fee. Agreement on fees contributes significantly to the success of a project and should be agreed in writing before work commences. Also check whether fees include VAT.

Designers work in various ways to produce a 'to scale' presentation plan – complete with plant list and build schedule – from which your garden can be built. Three-dimensional sketches may be included, and constructional sections and elevations to facilitate a build may be produced. It is important that you know exactly what you are paying the designer to produce, and the designer should be happy to supply written details of final delivery documentation in the initial quotation.

Once you are happy with your final design, you will be ready to get your garden built. Some designers will have a construction arm within their own company, but many choose to remain impartial. They may recommend reputable landscape contractors that they have worked with in the past, who will then be able to provide you with a quotation for their work. Again, choose your contractor with confidence; see facing page for further advice. Remember, during the garden build stage, it's a good idea to employ your designer to visit the site at intervals to make sure that the integrity and quality of the design is not compromised.

PREVIOUS PAGE *Repeating materials and plants in different areas gives the garden a cohesive look, which is especially important in a terraced space.*

EMPLOYING A LANDSCAPE CONTRACTOR

Finding a good landscape contractor (or, put more simply, 'garden installer') is essential, as you will rely on their advice, product knowledge and workmanship to achieve the garden you desire. Recommendation is the best way to find a good landscaping contractor – if friends or family have recently had work completed in their garden, find out if they would recommend the contractor involved. Ask whether they did a good job, worked within budget, were helpful, approachable and courteous. If they completed the work on time, were they tidy and considerate while on site? Did they identify and rectify any problem areas after the job was completed? If you see garden works being carried out locally and are impressed by the work that is going on, why not ask for a card. Similarly, if there is a garden you have admired, why not ask the homeowner for a recommendation. There are also several professional bodies, councils and manufacturers that have approved contractor lists, which should help you to find landscaping contractors in your area. An Internet or telephone directory search will provide details of local tradesmen – but be careful to check if they list membership of professional bodies in their advertizing. Finally, if you are using the services of a garden designer, they will certainly be able to recommend reputable contractors whom they regularly work with.

Always consider the following points when choosing a contractor:

Check if the company in question has a website. This will enable you to get a general feel for the company, and to see if their style of work is suitable for your project. It's important to check that the photographs on their website show examples of their own work.

Ask whether they have received any recommendations and can let you see their portfolio. Ask if it is possible to visit any gardens they have built in your local area.

You would expect a reputable contractor to be fully insured. They should also be happy to provide written quotations on headed paper with a VAT number, a landline telephone number (as opposed to a mobile), full address, and full terms and conditions.

Ask whether they offer a guarantee for their work. If so, find out how long it lasts and what it covers.

Ask how a job would usually run; would a team be on site throughout the entire build? Beware of a stop-start operation and check that a foreman will be on site at all times.

Enquire about their payment terms. Do they usually require a deposit (enquire about deposit guarantee schemes), and when would they expect their final sum to be paid? Check whether they are VAT registered.

Finally, enquire if after a site visit, receipt of a written quotation, and then agreement from yourselves, ask how quickly they could expect to begin the job, and how long they think the work will take, weather permitting. Reputable contractors are always busy, be wary of anyone who can start the next day.

I would always advise getting at least three written estimates for any job, making sure that all quotations received are on a like-for-like basis. Don't decide purely on price, choose the contractor that you feel comfortable with, and which best suits your needs – it may be the difference between a good job and an outstanding one.

BELOW *A colour link between the red* Crocosmia *in the foreground and the* Helenium *behind is enough to emphasise that this terraced garden is still one space.*

INDEX

Page references in *italics* refer to illustration captions

A

Acanthus
  A. mollis 54, 57, 61
  A. spinosus 29, 31
Acer palmatum dissectum
  'Atropurpureum' 29, 31
Achillea
  'Feuerland' 101, 103, 137, 139
  'Inca Gold' 71, 73
  'Moonshine' 136, 139
  A. millefolium 'Red Velvet' 71, 73
acid soil 173
Agapanthus 143
  'Blue Prince' 29, 30, 35
  Headbourne hybrids 71, 73, 121, 122, 137, 139
  'White Heaven' 29, 31
  A. campanulatus var. *albidus* 71, 73
Agastache 'Summer Love' 54, 57, 61, 101, 103
Ajuga reptans 71, 73
Akebia quinata 101, 102
Alcea rugosa 54, 57
Alchemilla mollis 12, 13, 19, 35, 54, 57, 60, 71, 73, 121, 122, 136, 137, 138, 139
alkaline soil 173
Allium
  'Purple Sensation' 54, 60, 61
  A. schoemoprasum 29, 31, 137, 139
American Landcress 29, 31
Anemanthele lessoniana 12, 13, 54, 57, 101, 103, 106, 121, 122, 136, 139
Anemone x *hybrida* 'Honorine Jobert' 121, 122
Angelica gigas 101, 103, 106
Anthriscus sylvestris 'Ravenswing' 101, 103
Aquilegia
  'Black Barlow' 136, 137, 138, 139
  'Ruby Port' 12, 13, 19, 136, 139
  'William Guinness' 137, 139
artichokes 29, 31, 34
Asplenium scolopendrium 137, 139
Astelia chathamica 71, 73, 77, 85, 90, 157
  'Silver Spear' 151, 152
Astrantia major 'Rubra' 29, 31

B

bamboo 12, 18, 85, 90, 143
barbecues 86, 89, 92
bark chip 100, 112
Batvia salad 29, 31
beans
  broad beans 101, 103
  climbing beans 29, 31
  dwarf French beans 101, 102
  French beans 29, 31
Bergenia cordifolia 136, 137, 139
  'Winterglut' 71, 73
Beta vulgaris 'Ruby Red' 29, 31
Blechnum spicant 121, 122, 137, 139
Blueberry 'Northsky' 29, 31
boundaries *see* fences; walls
broad beans 101, 103
Brunnera macrophylla 'Jack Frost' 29, 30, 35
Buxus sempervirens 101, 102, 110, 151, 152, 156

C

cabbages 29, 30, 31, *35*
Calamagrostis brachytricha 101, 103
Cannai sp. 121, 137, 139, 143
Carex pendula 121, 122
Carpinus betulus 71, 73
Ceanothus impressus 'Puget Blue' 136, 139
chalk soil 173
Chamaerops humilis 137, 139
Chilli 'Apache' 29, 31
Cirsium rivulare 'Atropurpureum' 121, 122
clay soil 173
Clematis
  'The President' 101, 102, 137
  C.. balearica 'Freckles' 137
Cobaea scandens 101, 102
Coereopsis verticillata 'Grandiflora' 101
compost, making 176
containers, preparing for planting 176
conuit pipes, laying 78
Cordyline australis 85, 90
Coreopsis verticillata 'Grandiflora' 101, 103
Cornus
  C. alba 'Aurea' 136, 139
  C. kousa chineses 'Rubra' 136, 139
Cosmos atrosanguineus 101, 102, *106*
courgettes 101, 103
Crocosmia
  'Emberglow' 137, 139
  'Emily McKenzie' 121, 122
  'George Davidson' 71, 73
  'Jackanapes' 101, 103
  'Lucifer' 136, 137, 139
  'Red King' 54, 57, 71, 73
  'Solfatare' 137, 139
cut-and-come-again salad 101, 103
Cynara cardunculus 34

D

Darmera peltata 121, 123, 127, 137, 139, 143
decking 164
  edible garden 28, 32, 36
  minimalist garden 152, 154, 158
  night garden 120, 125, 129
  rustic family garden 98, 100, 104–5, 110
  suntrap garden 70, 74, 78
  terraced garden 136, 144
  urban garden *10*, 16, 20
Deschampsia cespitosa 137, 139
  'Golden Dew' 12, 13, 19, *19*, 101, 103
designers, employing 180
Dicksonia antarctica 121, 122, 126, 137, 139, 143
Dierama pulcherrimum 101, 103
Digitalis
  'Alba' 101, 103
  'Camelot White' 29, 30, 35
  D. ferruginea 12, 13, 19, 54, 57, 60, 71, 73, 136
  D. grandiflora 19
dwarf French beans 101, 102

E

Echinacea purpurea
  'Magnus' 54, 57, 61, 71, 73, 77, 101, 103, 106, 121, 123
  'Rubinstern' 136, 139
Echinops ritro 'Veitch's Blue' 31
edging 37
edible garden
  hard landscaping 28, 32–3, 36–7
  maintenance 38–9
  method 36–7
  planning 26–31
  planting 29, 34–5, 37
electrics
  edible garden 36, 37
  low-maintenance garden 92
  minimalist garden 159
  night garden 129
  suntrap garden 79
English country garden
  hard landscaping 54, 58, 62
  maintenance 64
  method 62

planning 52–7
planting 54, 60–1, 62
Epimedium 35
Equisetum hyemale 121, 122, 127
Eryngium
    E. bourgatii 29, 31
    E. planum 'Blaukappe' 29, 31
Eunonymus fortunei 'Emerald 'n'
    Gold' 29, 31
Euphorbia
    E. amygdaloides 35
    E. amygdaloides 'Rubra' 137,
        139
    E. griffithii 'Dixter' 121, 123,
        136, 139
    E. mellifera 71, 73, 77, 137,
        139

F

Fatsia japonica 31
fencing 166–7
    edible garden 28, 32–3, 36
    low-maintenance garden 88
    suntrap garden 70, 74–5, 79
    urban garden 16, 20
Foeniculum vulgare 29, 31, 101,
    103
Forsythia x intermedia 'Spectablis'
    136, 138
French beans 29, 31, 101, 102
furniture 7
    edible garden 26
    English country garden 52, 58,
        60
    low-maintenance garden 89, 90,
        92
    minimalist garden 154–5, 158
    romantic front garden 48
    rustic family garden 100, 113
    urban garden 15

G

garden designers, employing 180
Gaura lindheimeri 12, 13, 18, 54,
    57, 136, 137, 138, 139
Geranium
    'Johnson's Blue' 136, 138, 139
    'Patricia' 43, 44, 47, 101, 103
    G. macrorrhizum 35
    G. macrorrhizum 'Bevan's
        Variety' 137, 139
Geum 'Fire Opal' 71, 73
glass aggregate concrete 124
Gleditsia triacanthos 'Sunburst'
    136, 139
grass *see* lawns
gravel 16, 32, 36, 37
    paths 28
greenhouses 142
Gunnera manicata 121, 122

H

Hamamelis mollis 136, 139
hard landscaping 6, 163–8
    edible garden 28, 32–3, 36–7
    English country garden 54, 58,
        62
    low-maintenance garden 86,
        88–9, 92
    minimalist garden 152, 154–5,
        158–9
    night garden 120, 124–5,
        128–9
    romantic front garden 44–6, 48
    rustic family garden 100,
        104–5, 110–13
    suntrap garden 68, 70, 74–5,
        78
    terraced garden 136, 140–2,
        144–5
    urban garden 10, 14–17
hazel hurdles 74–5, 79
Hedra helix 12
Hedychium
    H. coccineum 'Tara' 71, 73, 121
    H. gardnerianum 71, 73
Helenium
    'Moerheim Beauty' 101, 103,
        106, 136, 137, 139
    'Rubinzwerg' 71, 73, 77
    'Sahin's Early Flowerer' 29, 31,
        137, 139
Helianthus 'Lemon Queen' 136,
    137, 138, 139
Helleborus
    H. orientalis 12, 13
    H. x sternii 136, 137, 139
Hemerocallis
    'Hyperion' 137, 139
    'Ice Carnival' 12, 13, 19
    'Lemon Bells' 121, 122
    'Stafford' 54, 57, 60, 71, 73,
        76, 101, 137, 139
Heuchera
    'Crème Brûlée' 29, 31
    H. cylindrica 'Greenfinch' 71,
        73
    H. micrantha 'Purple Palace' 85,
        136, 139
Hosta
    'Patriot' 29, 31
    'Sum and Substance' 29, 30, 35
    'White Christmas' 137, 141
    H. fortunei 'Aureomarginata' 29,
        31
hot tub spas 136, 141, 144

I

Iris 'Quechee' 136, 138
irrigation 168
    low-maintenance garden 84, 86,
        89, 92

minimalist garden 152, 155,
    158, 159
night garden 120, 129
suntrap garden 70, 75, 79
urban garden 12, 20
Isotoma 'Dark Blue' 12, 13, 54, 57

K

Knautia macedonica 43, 44, 101,
    103, 136, 138, 139
Kniphofia 'Nancy's Red' 71, 73

L

landscape contractors employing
    181
Lathyrus odoratus sp. 29, 31
Laurus nobilis 29, 31, 137, 151,
    152, 157
Lavandula
    L. augustifolia 101, 103
    L. augustifolia 'Hidcote' 43, 44,
        44, 47, 54, 57, 60, 61,
        137, 139
    L. stoechas 29, 31
lawns
    low-maintenance garden 84–6
    romantic front garden 46
    rustic family garden 112
    terraced garden 141, 145
    urban garden 12, 16
Leucanthemum 'Highland White
    Dream' 29, 31
Liatris spicata 54, 57, 101, 103
lighting 7, 168
    edible garden 28, 33
    low-maintenance garden 84, 86,
        89, 92
    minimalist garden 152, 155,
        158
    night garden 118, 120, 125,
        129
    suntrap garden 70, 75
    urban garden 12, 20
Ligularia dentata 'Desdemona' 29,
    31
Ligustrum
    L. delavayanum 137
    L. jonandrum 43, 44, 47
loam 173
Lonicera
    L. japonica 'Hall's Prolific' 137
    L. periclymenum 'Belgica' 101,
        102, 121
    L. periclymenum 'Graham
        Thomas' 101, 102
low-maintenance garden
    hard landscaping 86, 88–9, 92
    maintenance 94
    method 92
    planning 84–6

planting 86, 90, 92
Luzula nivea 137, 139
Lychnis
   L. chalcedonica 101, 103
   L. flos-cuculi 121, 122
Lysimachia ciliata 'Firecracker' 71, 73, 76

M

maintenance
   edible garden 38–9
   English country garden 64
   low-maintenance garden 94
   minimalist garden 160
   night garden 130
   romantic front garden 49
   rustic family garden 114–15
   suntrap garden 80
   terraced garden 146–7
   urban garden 22
Matteuccia struthiopteris 121, 122
method
   edible garden 36–7
   English country garden 62
   low-maintenance garden 92
   minimalist garden 158–9
   night garden 128–9
   romantic front garden 48
   rustic family garden 110–13
   suntrap garden 78–9
   terraced garden 144–5
   urban garden 20–1
Mimulus 'Bonfire Red' 121, 122
minimalist garden
   hard landscaping 152, 154–5, 158–9
   maintenance 160
   method 158–9
   planning 150–2
   planting 152, 156–7, 159
mint 31
mirrors 120, 125
Miscanthus
   'Gracillimus' 54, 57, 101, 103
   M. sinensis 'Ferner Osten' 101, 102
   M. sinensis 'Malepartus' 71, 73, 77, 136, 139
misters 124
Monarda
   'Cambridge Scarlet' 101, 103
   'Mahogany' 136, 138
   'Scorpion' 43, 44, 54, 57, 60, 101, 103, 106, *107*
Musa basjoo 137, 139, *141*
Mustard 'Green Frills' 29, 31

N

Nemesia 'Confetti' 12, 13, 54, 57
Nepeta

'Bramdean' 54, 57
'Six Hills Giant' 136, 139
'Walker's Low' 101, 103
N. sibirica 'Souvenir d'André Chaudron' 54, 57
Nicotiana sylvestris 29, 31
night garden
   hard landscaping 120, 124–5, 128–9
   maintenance 130
   method 128–9
   planning 118–23
   planting 121, 126–7, 129

O

Olea euripaea 12
olive trees 18, *21*
Ophiopogon planiscapus 'Nigrescens' 121, 122, 123
Origanum laevigatum 'Herrenhausen' 54, 57, 61, 101, 103
Oxalis 'Sunset Velvet' 71, 73

P

Parthenocissus
   P. henryana 121, 123, 137, 139
   P. quinquefolia 29, 30
Passiflora caerulea 121, 137, 139
paths 28, 32, 36, *37*
paving 163
   English country garden 54, 58, 62
   low-maintenance garden 86, 88–9, 92
   minimalist garden 152, 155, 159
   romantic front garden 44, 46, 48
   suntrap garden 70, 74, 78
   terraced garden 136, 144
   urban garden 12, 14–15, 21
Pennisetum alopecuroides 'Hameln' 101, 103
pergolas 52, 58, 136, 142, 144
Perpetual Spinach 29, 31
Persicaria
   P. affinis 'Superba' 54, 57, 61
   P. amplexicaulis 'Atrosanguinea' 71, 73, 77, 137, 139
   P. filiforme 137, 139
Phlomis russeliana 137, 139
Phormium
   'Flamingo' 29, 31, 143
   'Platt's Black' 71, 73, 76
   'Yellow Wave' 137, 139
Phyllostachys
   P. aurea 12, 18, 29

P. nigra 12, 13, 85, 90, 101, 102, 121, 122, 137, 139, 143
pipes, laying 78
planning 173–81
   edible garden 26–31
   English country garden 52–7
   low-maintenance garden 84–6
   minimalist garden 150–2
   night garden 118–23
   romantic front garden 42–5
   rustic family garden 98–103
   suntrap garden 68–73
   terraced garden 134–9
   urban garden 10–13
planning regulations
   decking 16
   fencing 16
   paving 15
planting
   edible garden 29, 34–5, 37
   English country garden 54, 60–1, 62
   low-maintenance garden 86, 90, 92
   minimalist garden 152, 156–7, 159
   night garden 121, 126–7, 129
   romantic front garden 44, 47, 48
   rustic family garden 101, 106–7, 112–13
   suntrap garden 71, 76–7, 79
   terraced garden 136–7, 143, 145
   urban garden 12–13, 18–19, 21
Platycodon grandiflorus 12, 13, 54, 57
Polystichum setiferum 29, 35
potatoes 101, 103
   ' Duke of York' 29, 31
   'Charlotte' 29
Potentilla
   'Gibson's Scarlet' 71, 73, 76
   'Red Ace' 122
potting sheds 33, 37
Primula bulleyana 121, 122

R

railway sleepers 113, 140–1
raised vegetable boxes 28, 32, 34–5, 37
rhubarb 'Glaskins Perpetual' 29, 31
Robina pseudoacacia 'Frisia' 29, 30
Rodgersia pinnata 137, 139, 143
romantic front garden
   hard landscaping 44–6, 48
   maintenance 49
   method 48
   planning 42–5

planting 44, 47, 48
Rosmarinus officinalis 29, 31, 85
    'Miss Jessop's Upright' 12
Rudbeckia
    R. fulgida deamii 121, 122
    R. fulgida 'Goldsturm' 71, 73,
    77
rustic family garden
    hard landscaping 100, 104–5,
    110–13
    maintenance 114–15
    method 110–13
    planning 98–103
    planting 101, 106–7, 112–13

S

Salvia
    S. nemorosa 101, 103
    S. nemorosa 'Ostfriesland' 137,
    139
    S. officinalis 137, 138
    S. officinalis 'Tricolor' 29, 31
Sambucus nigra 'Guincho Purple'
    137, 138
sandy soil 173
Sanguisorba obtusa 101, 103
Santolina chamaecyparissus 101,
    103
scale plans 175
screening *see* trellis
seating areas *see* furniture
Sedum
    'Autumn Joy' 121, 122
    'Gooseberry Fool' 54, 57
    'Herbstfreude' 101, 103, 137,
    139
sett paths 32, 36
shade sails 120, 125
sheds 33, 37
Sisyrinchium striatum 101, 103,
    137, 139
soil, preparing 173
Soleirolia soleirolii 12, 14, 15, 19,
    121, 122, 126
Sorbus aria 12, 13, 101
spinach 29, 31
Stachys monieri 'Hummelo' 101,
    103
staircases 124, 129
Star Jasmine 12, 13, 19, *19*
steps *16*
    English country garden 58
    rustic family garden 100,
    110–12

terraced garden 136
Stipa
    S. gigantea 54, 57, 71, 101,
    103, 106
    S. tenuissima 54, 57, 60, 73,
    106, 137, 139
summerhouses 124
sunflowers 101, 103, 107
suntrap garden
    hard landscaping 68, 70, 74–5,
    78
    maintenance 80
    method 78–9
    planning 68–73
    planting 71, 76–7, 79
sweet peas 101, 102, *107*
sweetcorn 'Swift' 29, 31
Swiss chard 'Bright Lights' 29, 31
Syringa vulgaris 'Madame Antoine
    Buchner' 137, 138

T

Tellima grandiflora 137, 139
terraced garden
    hard landscaping 136, 140–2,
    144–5
    maintenance 146–7
    method 144–5
    planning 134–9
    planting 136–7, 143, 145
terraces
    English country garden 58
    rustic family garden 98
    terraced garden 136, 141, 144
Thymus
    T. coccineus 54, 57
    T. vulgaris 29, 31
Tiarella cordifolia 29, 31
tomatoes 29, 31, 101, 102
Trachelospermum jasminoides 12,
    13, 19, *19*, 43, 44, *44*, 47,
    71, 73, 101, 102, 106,
    121, 123, 137, 142, 143
Trachycarpus fortunei 121, 122,
    126, 137, 139, 143
trampolines 105, 112
trellis
    minimalist garden 152, 154,
    158
    night garden 120
    urban garden 12, 16, 20
Trifolium rubens 101, 103
Tropaeolum majus 'Jewel Mixed'
    29, 30, 35

U

urban garden
    hard landscaping 12, 14–17,
    20–1
    maintenance 22
    method 20–1
    planning 10–13
    planting 12–13, 18–19, 21

V

vegetables *see* edible garden;
    rustic family garden
Verbena bonariensis 29, 43, 44,
    47, 54, 57, 61, 71, 73,
    101, 103, 121, 137
Veronicastrum virginicum
    'Fascination' 101, 103
    'Temptation' 71, 73, 101, 103
Viola labradorica 54, 57, 60
Vitis coignetiae 121, 122, 123

W

walls
    minimalist garden 152, 154
    romantic front garden 44, 48
    rustic family garden 100, 104,
    110
    suntrap garden 75, 78
    terraced garden 136, 140–1
    urban garden 12, 16, 20
water features
    night garden 120, 124
    terraced garden 142, 144
watering systems *see* irrigation
Weigela florida 'Variegata' 137,
    139
Wisteria sinensis 43, 44, 47, 57

X

x *Fatshedera lizei* 29, 30, 35

Z

Zantedeschia aethiopica
    'Crowborough' 29, 30, 35,
    121, 122, 123

LIST OF SUPPLIERS

CONTRACTORS

The Garden Builders
259 Munster Road
Fulham
London
SW6 6BW
Tel: 020 7381 8002
www.gardenbuilders.co.uk

Garden House Design
4 Roundstone Barn
Roundstone Farm
Littlehampton Road
Worthing
BN12 6PW
Tel: 01903 774 774
www.gardenhousedesign
.co.uk

MATERIALS

Travis Perkins
Head Office:
Lodge Way House
Lodge Way
Harlestone Road
Northampton
NN5 7UG
Tel: 01604 752 424
www.travisperkins.co.uk

Build Centre
Head Office:
Wolseley UK
The Wolseley Center
Harrison Way
Spa Park
Royal Leamington Spa
CV31 3HH
Tel: 0800 529 529
www.buildcenter.co.uk

Jewson
Head Office:
Merchant House
Binley Business Park
Coventry
CV3 2TT
Tel: 024 7643 8400
www.jewson.co.uk

Marshalls
Landscape House
Premier Way
Lowfields Business Park
Elland
HX5 9HT
Tel: 0845 820 5000
www.marshalls.co.uk

StoneMarket
Oxford Road
Ryton on Dunsmore
Warwickshire
CV8 3EJ
Tel: 024 7651 8700
www.stonemarket.co.uk

Benton Weatherstone
53 Ferringham Lane
Ferring
Worthing
West Sussex
BN12 5NT
Tel: 01903 243202
www.bentonweatherstone
.co.uk

Specialist Aggregates
162 Cannock Road
Stafford
ST17 0QJ
Tel: 01785 665 554
www.specialistaggregates
.co.uk

FENCING

Hillhout
OLG U.K.
Unit 3A
Red House Farm
Wood Walton
Huntingdon
Cambridgeshire
PE28 5YL
Tel: 01487 772 901
www.hillhout.eu

AVS fencing
Head Office:
Unit 1, The Courtyard
Pondtail Farm
Buckbarn, West
Grinstead
West Sussex
RH13 8LN
Tel: 01403 740 200
www.avsfencing.co.uk

Forest Garden
Unit 291 & 296
Hartlebury Trading Estate
Hartlebury
Worcestershire
DY10 4JB
Tel: 0844 248 9801
www.forestgarden.co.uk

TIMBER

English Woodlands Timber
Cocking Sawmills
Cocking
Near Midhurst
West Sussex
GU29 0HS
Tel:01730 816 941
www.ewtimber.co.uk

Silva Timber Products
Wyevale Garden Centre
Pield Heath Road
Hillingdon
Middlesex
UB8 3NP
Tel: 01895 271 300
www.decksupply.co.uk

FinnForest
Head Office:
46 Berth
Tilbury Freeport
Tilbury
Essex
RM18 7HS
Tel: 01375 856 855
www.finnforest.co.uk

Alsford Timber
Head Office:
Ness Road
Erith
Kent
DA8 2LD
Tel: 01322 333 088
www.alsfordtimber.com

Railway Sleeper
Owthorpe Rd
Cotgrave
Nottingham
NG12 3PU
Tel: 0115 9890 445
www.railwaysleeper.com

LIGHTING

Lighting for Gardens
7 Dunhams Court
Letchworth Garden City
Hertfordshire
SG6 1WB
Tel: 01462 486 777
www.lightingforgardens.com

Hunza (Europe)

Light Ideas International
Ltd & Hunza Europe
Suite No.3
Faraday House
King William Street
Amblecote
Stourbridge
DY8 4HD
Tel: 01384 377 378
www.hunzaeurope.com

Collingwood Lighting

Brooklands House
Sywell Aerodrome
Wellingborough Road
Sywell
Northampton
NN6 0BT
Tel: 01604 495151
www.collingwoodlighting
.com

NURSERIES

Aldingbourne

Church Road
Aldingbourne
Chichester
PO20 3TU
Tel: 0800 085 7970
www.aldingbournenurseries
.co.uk

Orchard Dene Nurseries

Lower Assendon
Henley-on-Thames
Oxfordshire
RG8 6AG
Tel: 01491 575 075
www.orcharddene.co.uk

Tendercare

Southlands Road
Denham
Uxbridge
Middlesex
UB9 4HD
Tel: 01895 835 544
www.tendercare.co.uk

Hillier

Head Office:
The Stables
Ampfield House
Ampfield
Romsey
Hampshire
SO51 9BQ
Tel: 01794 368 733
www.hillier.co.uk

Crocus (online company)

Tel: 0844 557 2233
www.crocus.co.uk

IRRIGATION AND WATER FEATURES

Hozelock

Midpoint Park
Birmingham
B76 1AB
Tel: 0121 313 1122
www.hozelock.com

Stowasis

Woodside House
Sidings Court
Doncaster
DN4 5NU
Tel: 01302 767 170
www.stowasis.com

GARDEN ACCESSORIES

Barbed Ltd

3 Liffords Place
Barnes High Street
Barnes
London
SW13 9LR
Tel: 020 88781 994
www.barbedltd.co.uk

Bright Green

65 Byfield Road
Woodford Halse
Northants
NN11 3QR
Tel: 01327 263 777
www.brightgreen.co.uk

Whichford Pottery

Whichford
Near Shipston-on-Stour
Warwickshire
CV36 5PG
Tel: 01608 684 416
www.whichfordpottery.com

Iota Garden an Home Limited

Wick Road
Wick St Lawrence
North Somerset
BS22 7YQ
Tel: 01934 522 617
www.iotagarden.com

GLOSSARY

Balau A tropical hardwood timber often manufactured and used for decking boards.

Bract A specialized leaf growing just below a flower. They can be inconspicuous or showy and petal-like.

Coping stone A protective stone used to protect a wall from weather. It can also be used to give a decorative finish.

Ericaceous compost A lime-free compost used to promote the growth of acid-loving plants such as azalea, camellia and rhododendron.

Fish, blood and bone A slow-release general plant fertilizer, often organic.

Gabions Whicker or metal cages filled with earth or stone. They are used regularly in landscaping as a method of retaining slopes but can also be decorative.

Geotextile membrane A woven garden fabric most often used for weed control, ground stabilizing, drainage, filtration and tree-root protection.

Grazing lights Grazing is a term used to describe a light that is angled on a surface to accentuate texture.

Hardcore layer A layer of broken material used as the bottom layer of patio foundations.

Haunch A method of applying mortar to retain hard landscaping. Applied to kerbs, edging materials and so on.

Humus Decomposed organic matter from plant material for use as compost. Often found naturally as a soil layer in woodlands.

Joist beam Supporting beams used in decking to support boards.

Nematode Microscopic creatures, many of whose larvae feed on common garden pests without harming beneficial insects, worms or birds. Used as organic pest control.

Panicles A branched cluster of flowers, for example *Buddleja*.

Point A term used for filling the gaps between paving materials with mortar.

Portland cement The most common type of cement in use today.

Potager A kitchen garden of vegetables, herbs and fruits, laid out ornamentally.

Scalpings The chippings left over from stonework and sold for use in patio and path foundations.

Screed The final smooth coat used to render walling or concrete flooring.

Setts Cubes of landscape stone such as granite or sandstone used as paving material.

Solenoid valve A valve used in an automatic irrigation system to control the flow of water.

Stringers The side sections of a ladder step system used to support the step treads.

Tamp A term used to describe the packing down of patio foundations or concrete in order to knock out air.

Tanalised A term used for timber that has been preserved by impregnating it with chemicals applied under pressure.

Yorkstone A popular, traditional English sandstone used in garden landscaping.

FURTHER READING

Alexander, Rosemary. *The Essential Garden Design Workbook* (Timber Press, 2004)

Archer-Wills, Anthony. *The Water Gardener* (Frances Lincoln, 2000)

Blanc, Alan. *Landscape Construction and Detailing* (McGraw-Hill Inc., 1996)

Bradley-Hole, Christopher. *The Minimalist Garden* (Mitchell Beazley, 1999)

Brickell, Christopher. *The RHS Essential Garden Planning and Construction* (Mitchell Beazley, 2006)

Brookes, John. *John Brookes Garden Design Course* (Mitchell Beazley, 2007)

Chatto, Beth. *Beth Chatto's Green Tapestry: Perennial Plants For Your Garden* (Harper Collins Illustrated, 1999)

Church, Thomas D. *Gardens are for People* (University of California Press, 1995)

Compton, Tania, and Andrew Lawson. *Dream Gardens: 100 Inspirational Gardens* (Merrell Publishers Ltd., 2007)

Conran, Terence, and Dan Pearson. *The Essential Garden Book: The Comprehensive Source Book of Garden Design* (Conran Octopus Ltd., 2001)

Cooper, Paul. *The New Tech Garden* (Mitchell Beazley, 2007)

Don, Monty. *Extraordinary Gardens of the World* (Weidenfeld & Nicolson, 2009)

King, Michael, and Piet Oudolf. *Gardening with Grasses* (Frances Lincoln, 1998)

Littlewood, Michael. *Landscape Detailing, Volume 1: Enclosures* (Architectural Press, 1993)

Littlewood, Michael. *Landscape Detailing, Volume 2: Surfaces* (Architectural Press, 1993)

Littlewood, Michael. *Landscape Detailing, Volume 3: Structures* (Architectural Press, 1997)

Littlewood, Michael. *Landscape Detailing, Volume 4: Water* (Architectural Press, 2001)

Lloyd, Christopher. *Christopher Lloyd's Garden Flowers: Perennials, Bulbs, Grasses, Ferns* (Timber Press, 2000)

Lloyd, Christopher. *Succession Planting for Adventurous Gardeners* (BBC Books, 2005)

Oudolf, Piet, and Henk Gerritsen. *Planting the Natural Garden* (Timber Press, 2003)

Powell, Ann-Marie. *Hard Landscaping for the Garden* (David & Charles Plc., 2003)

Powell, Ann-Marie. *Urban Gardens* (Cassell Illustrated, 2005)

Raine, John. *Garden Lighting: Design, Inspiration, Techniques* (Hamlyn, 2005)

Raven, Sarah. *The Bold and Brilliant Garden* (Frances Lincoln, 2001)

Sturgeon, Andy. *Planted* (Soma Books, 1998)

Swift, Joe. *Joe's Urban Garden Handbook* (Quadrille Publishing Ltd., 2008)

Swindells, Philip and David Mason. *The Complete Book of the Water Garden* (Cassell Illustrated, 1992)

Williams , Robin, Mary-Jane Hopes and Robin Templar Williams. *The Complete Book of Patio and Container Gardening* (Cassell Illustrated, 2001)

Wilson, Andrew. *The Book of Garden Plans* (Mitchell Beazley, 2004)

ACKNOWLEDGEMENTS

I would like to thank my clients who commissioned me to design their gardens in the first place, and without whom this book would certainly not have existed – in no particular order they are Lucy Cufflin and Ian Coleby, Rachel and Simon Perry, Ian and Eve Archer, Bev and Kev Xhevis, Nick Fox and Ana Lopez, Paul and Caroline Leech, Nick and Katrina Swift, Delianne Forget, and Pat and Gill Ashby. I'd also like to thank all those at Anova Books, most especially Emily Preece-Morrison, Anna Cheifetz (both presently on maternity leave) and the thankfully unimpregnable David Salmo!

Heartfelt thanks also to the talented and creative Rachel Warne, not only for her beautiful photography but also for her energy, enthusiasm and fun. Introduced by our mutual friend James Alexander-Sinclair (thanks to you too my darling!) who thought we might work well together on this book, we have since become firm friends, though all around us now wish that James had also included a volume control at our initial introduction.

I'd like to thank Mark and Rod Winrow of Garden House Design, and also Neil Dunster of The Garden Builders for being brilliantly skilled builders, and also great friends, and, of course, I should like to pass on my thanks to everyone in their landscaping teams, who have all been such a pleasure to work with.

I should like to send thanks to all the nurseries that have supplied such stunning plants to me over the years – Chris and Toby Marchant at Orchard Dene, Steve McIntyre at Aldingbourne Nurseries and Gordon Catlin at Manor Farm Nurseries.

I'd also like to thank my friends for patiently encouraging me to sit down and just write (especially John Anthony Conlon for his many words of wisdom!), and all the underground gardeners for, well, just being them (you know who you are).

And I'd like to thank my family, especially Alice Bundy for being my children's perfect second-mummy-granny-nanny, allowing me to keep my career going whilst not worrying about the amount of love and attention my children are receiving at home. Jules, Archie, Gilbert and I love you so very much.

And Jules Bundy, for being my right-hand man in everything I do, both at work and at home, thank you so much for your friendship, your love and your support in my career and also my life. I love you babe.

And finally to Archie for being my favourite eldest son, and to Gilbert, my favourite youngest son, who was conceived, born, and breastfed throughout the writing of this book. Thanks for being such wonderful, snugly, patient, happy children.